AF539316

India and the European Union in a Changing World

India and the European Union in a Changing World

Edited by

Rajendra K. Jain

India and the European Union in a Changing World
Edited by Rajendra K. Jain

© Authors for the respective chapters
© Editor

First Published, 2014

ISBN 978-93-5002-263-4

All rights reserved. No part of this book may be reproduced
or transmitted, in any form or by any means, without
prior permission of the Publisher.

Published by
AAKAR BOOKS
28 E Pocket IV, Mayur Vihar Phase I, Delhi 110 091
Phone : 011 2279 5505 Telefax : 011 2279 5641
info@aakarbooks.com; www.aakarbooks.com

Printed at
Saurabh Printers Pvt. Ltd., A 16, Sector IV, Noida

Contents

List of Figures

List of Tables

List of Abbreviations

ACP	Africa, Caribbean and the Pacific
AfT	Aid for Trade
ASEAN	Association of South East Asian Nations
ASEM	Asia Europe Meeting
AWG-LCA	Ad Hoc Working Group on Long-term Cooperation Action
CCIT	Comprehensive Convention on International Terrorism
CFSP	Common Foreign and Security Policy
CLMV	Cambodia, Laos, Myanmar and Vietnam
CSP	Country Strategy Paper
DAC	Development Assistance Committee
DCI	Development Cooperation Investment
DFID	Department for International Development
EBA	Everything but Arms
EC	European Commission
ECBC	Energy Conservation Building Code
ECCP	European Climate Change Programme
ECHO	European Community Humanitarian Office
ECOSOC	Economic and Social Committee
EDF	European Development Fund
FDI	Foreign Direct Investment
FTA	Free Trade Agreement
GATT	General Agreement on Tariffs and Trade

GAVI	Global Alliance for Vaccines and Immunization
GFATM	Global Fund to Fight AIDS, Tuberculosis and Malaria
GHG	Greenhouse Gas
GSP	General System of Preferences
ICAO	International Civil Aviation Organization
IMF	International Monetary Fund
IPCC	Intergovernmental Panel on Climate Change
IREDA	Indian Renewable Energy Development Agency Ltd.
JAP	Joint Action Plan
LDCs	Least Developed Countries
MDGs	Millennium Development Goals
MIP	Multi-Annual National Indicative Programme
NATO	North Atlantic Treaty Organization
NIEO	New International Economic Order
OECD	Organization for Economic Cooperation and Development
PIIGS	Portugal, Ireland, Italy, Greece and Spain
R2P	Responsibility to Protect
RBI	Reserve Bank of India
SIP	Sector Investment Programme
UN	United Nations
UNFCC	United Nations Framework Convention on Climate Change
WTO	World Trade Organization

Contributors

Jayaraj Amin is Professor of International Relations, Department of Political Science, Mangalore University, Mangalore.

Sachin Chaturvedi is Senior Fellow, Research and Information System for the Non-aligned and Developing Countries, a think tank of the Government of India's Ministry of External Affairs.

Pramit Pal Chaudhuri is Foreign Editor, *Hindustan Times*, New Delhi. He was formerly a member of the National Security Advisory Board (2011-2013).

Hartmut Elsenhans is Professor Emeritus of International Relations, Institute of Political Science, Leipzig University.

V.G. Hegde is Associate Professor, Faculty of Legal Studies, South Asia University, New Delhi. He was formerly Associate Professor, Centre for International Legal Studies, School of International Studies, Jawaharlal Nehru University, New Delhi (2004-2012).

Rajendra K. Jain is Professor, Centre for European Studies, School of International Studies, Jawaharlal Nehru University, New Delhi and the first and only Jean Monnet Chair in India. He is also Adjunct Professor (Research), Monash European and EU Studies Centre, Monash

University, Melbourne. He was formerly Visiting Humboldt Foundation Professor at Constance, Freiburg, Leipzig and Tübingen universities in Germany and Visiting Professor, the Maison des Sciences de l'Homme, Paris, and the Asia-Europe Institute, University of Malaya. He is the author/editor of over 30 books and 100 journal articles/book chapters.

Karina Jædrzejowska is Assistant Professor, Institute of International Relations, University of Warsaw.

B. Krishnamoorthy is Associate Professor, Department of Political Science and International Relations, and Director, Centre for European Studies, Pondicherry University, Pondicherry.

Satish Nambiar was formerly Director, United Service Institute, New Delhi and first Force Commander and Head of Mission of the United Nations forces in the former Yugoslavia (1992-1993).

Archna Negi is Assistant Professor, Centre for International Politics, Organization and Disarmament, School of International Studies, Jawaharlal Nehru University, New Delhi.

Gulshan Sachdeva is Chairperson and Professor, Centre for European Studies, School of International Studies, Jawaharlal Nehru University, New Delhi.

Preface

Relations between India and the European Union have considerably widened and deepened beyond the traditional trade and economic orientation since the launch of the strategic partnership nearly a decade ago. This volume makes a significant contribution to the growing discussion on the multifarious economic, political, and security challenges that India-EU relations confront in a changing world.

This book is a collection of papers presented at the international conference on "India and the European Union in a Changing World: Perceptions and Perspectives" organized at the School of International Studies, Jawaharlal Nehru University on 1-2 March 2012. The seminar and publication of this volume was made possible under Grant No. 2010-3113 for the JNU Jean Monnet Chair from the Lifelong Learning Programme of the European Commission. This volume reflects the views only of the contributors, and the Commission cannot be held responsible for any use which may be made of the information contained therein.

Rajendra K. Jain

1

India, Europe and the Rise of Asia

Pramit Pal Chaudhuri

The European Union's engagement with Asia has been over 40 years in the making. However, besides the obvious trade and investment issues, Europe continues to struggle to find traction in the other part of Eurasia. Throughout Asia, strategic and political calculations barely factor in Europe – and never the European Union.

The European Union's most promising relationship was a roughly decade-long wooing of China. Today, even those European scholars and diplomats who welcomed the rise of a special relationship between Brussels and Beijing accept that it was at best a mirage. Europe was taken for a ride by China. It is not taken seriously by India. And it is taken as alien to Asian regionalism. This beggars the question: Why?

While there are obvious structural issues that bedevil Europe's relations with Asia, there are also far more fundamental problems in terms of differing worldviews. The first structural problem is simply geography. Europe and Asia are connected by land – but a huge sparsely populated expanse of it mostly controlled by the Commonwealth of Independent States, but not by sea. And that has made all the difference in areas like security.

The second structural problem is Brussels versus the Rest.

Even a journalist, like myself, has had the experience of officials from some of the governments of the largest European states explaining how they would like New Delhi to support their national policies – so they could undermine the policy being pushed by Brussels. But the core problem of the Europe and Asia relationship goes much deeper.

The nations of Europe have ordered their polity in a way that the British scholar-diplomat Robert Cooper, among others, has called "postmodern". From this has flowed a distinct worldview, including a unique view of how security is best accomplished and the role of sovereignty in the international system.[1]

What is striking is that this worldview could not be more different, and arguably more baffling, than the modernist stance that holds among most Asian nations. If anything, this modern worldview, similar to the post-Westphalian system accepted by the Western world without question until the end of the Cold War, is hardening in Asia.

The post-Westphalian state structure that arose in Europe – and later spread to most of the world – was designed to prevent the genocidal chaos of the Thirty Years' War. It had three key consequences.

First, it made the nation-state the building block of the international system. The domestic affairs of such states should be treated as sovereign, immune to the external interference of others. Without this rule, it was assumed, conflict over universal concepts like religion and ideology, wars that could rage on forever, would be legitimized.

Second, as a consequence, the favoured system of tackling the ever-changing power structure of nation-states became the balance of power. The balance of power carried an implicit threat of violence. And, unsurprisingly, it had to show this iron fist inside the glove of diplomacy and ensured that wars broke out on a regular basis – but wars that had clearer rules and which sought ultimately to restore the nation-state system.

Third, a "sovereignty first" standard and the balance of power meant that states were given a free ride on moral and ethical issues. A government was different from an individual because it had things like the balance of power to maintain. It could do dirty and covert things, commit murders and theft, and so on that would put a normal person behind bars.[2] This became accepted as the way the world should be run. Until the European experience of the two World Wars. This trauma, the historical literature of which would fill a library or a couple of large hard drives, led Europeans to conclude that the post-Westphalian system had outlived its shelf life. The Cold War, in many ways the same balance of power writ large and underpinned by the threat of nuclear annihilation, did little to change this sentiment.

The political philosophy that lay behind the creation of the European Union had a radically different concept of how relations between nations should be ordered. It overturned all three of the pillars of the Westphalian system mentioned previously. First, it argued that while the nation-state would remain an important method of political organization, it would not be seen as the brick and mortar of the regional order. Governments would not receive special sovereignty-based favours, the right to wage war and a waiver on acts of questionable morality. A national government, at the very least, would be held to the same standards as a provincial or municipal body.

This was explicit from the start. In one of the drafts of the Schuman Plan, Jean Monnet wrote, "This proposal has an essential political objective: to make a breach in the ramparts of national sovereignty."[3]

Second, as a consequence, the favoured way to handle relations between national governments was transparency and mutual agreed interference. The European states would poke inside each other's affairs. They would open their military systems to inspection, combination and eventual union. As it has been said, "Mutual interference is normal for postmodern states."[4] It also meant that "Of the big powers, only the European Union can be relied on to champion multilateralism."[5]

Throughout the 1980s and 1990s, the pace of European unity was actually breathtaking. The end of the Cold War allowed Europe to take apart one of the world's most entrenched defence systems – of which the Berlin Wall was only a small and visible component. The consolidation of standards, judicial systems, creation of a single continental parliament and, finally, the fusion of seventeen independent monetary policies were done on a timeline unsurpassed in history. These all carry a "still under construction" sign on them, but they are almost certainly here to stay. Including, despite the problems that have beset it since 2009, the Euro.

Europeans have rightly taken pride in this. More importantly, they can claim – as no other region in the world can claim barring possibly North America – that war and violent conflict in their region has been relegated to the dustbin of history. However, the violent breakup of Yugoslavia and the existence of more traditional, modern nation-states on their borders like Russia and Turkey, has led Europe to accept they cannot rest on their laurels. To preserve the success of the European model, the model had to spread beyond its borders.

There were reasons for Europe to believe this was do-able. It had successfully democratized the military-fascist rules of southern Europe. It had absorbed and transformed the communist states of Eastern Europe. And, though the task is hardly finished, it is inexorably moderating the volatile tribalism of the southern Slavs.

The European Union and China

The highpoint of pan-European optimism was the belief that developed in the period running from 1994 to 2008 that the European Union could serve, and would be accepted, as a model for an emerging China. In hindsight, this sounds like hubris on the scale of the Tower of Babel – which, it may be remembered, had been an attempt by a united human race to make a structure that would touch heaven and be seen from anywhere in the world. This European policy arose because the EU concluded in 1995 that it needed "a long-term strategy that reflects China's worldwide, as well as regional, economic and political influence." This followed from a belief that future Europe's own future competitiveness needed stronger economic ties and the credibility of the EU's own foreign policy required a "coherent China strategy".[6] But its 1995 strategy ambitiously said that Brussels first objective was to "socialize China into the kind of international order that the EU supports." This included non-proliferation, support for the United Nations, global environmental issues and so on. Its second objective was to help China's internal transition in areas like reducing regional disparities, green policies and civil society support.

EU officials spoke of how China and the EU "face similar problems and favour similar approaches to solving them." One Eurocrat, speaking about Brussels' assistance to China's domestic problems, said, "Officially, we call it 'exchange of experience,' but in reality we are exporting our model to China."[7]

The Europeans believed that enmeshing China into a network of international obligations and exposing it to the European way of doing things, would make China easier to "manage" and make it less likely to be a revisionist power.[8]

There was much scepticism by the US and definitely among most of China's Asian neighbours of the entire European view that China was a "status quo power that will be primarily preoccupied with its own internal challenges for the foreseeable future – a bit like the EU itself".[9]

Brussels may have been partially blinded by the economic carrots that Beijing waved. Premier Li Peng in 1996 said, "If the Europeans worked with China in all areas, not all economically but also politically and in other areas, I think they would get more contracts with China." But Beijing almost from the word go stoutly resisted any agreement on "common values", migration policy and intellectual property rights. The China 2003 Policy Paper on EU made it clear that human rights discussions should be kept to "social and economic rights".[10] Anything political was off the agenda. By then Human Rights Watch, among others, was denouncing the EU-China human rights dialogue as an "empty shell".

By 2007 even the economic relationship began souring as the European Union racked up massive trade deficits with China that it blamed, like the US, on Beijing's careful tilting of the business and trade environment. European firms, especially in the luxury goods and engineering sectors, complained of their products being pirated by Chinese goods – and Beijing's lack of redress on these issues.

By 2009 the human rights issues were becoming an issue even with the European Street. China's support for the Sudanese government over the Darfur massacres led to public protests. The final straw was the repression of the Tibetan riots that year, heavy-handed Chinese attempts to control the Olympic torch relay, and the subsequent reaction to the protests of Muslim minority members in Xinjiang. Europeans, who had once placed the US as the biggest threat to global security following the invasions of Iraq and Afghanistan, replaced Washington with Beijing.[11] A 2009 US-European discussion about the state of Europe's dialogue with China on human rights was suitably dismal with Bejing using every possible device to block any discussion on political rights and rule of law.[12] The principle on which the European strategy of engagement-in-depth towards China began to come apart.

An exhaustive analysis of the EU's relationship with China by the European Council of Foreign Affairs in 2009 was particularly hard-hitting. "The EU's China strategy is based on an anachronistic belief that China, under the influence of

European engagement, will liberalise its economy, improve the rule of law and democratize its politics." Instead, it said, "China's foreign and domestic policy has evolved in a way that has paid little heed to European values, and today Beijing regularly contravenes or even undermines them."[13] Far from being a catalyst for change in China, the report said, the EU's policy had become one of "unconditional engagement" where Europe unilaterally gave China access to its markets and provided it investments and received nothing in return.

The Chinese, the report argues, showed remarkable skill in playing the various European countries against each other and undermining any possibility of a continental approach to Beijing. China treats the "relationship with the EU as a game of chess, with 27 opponents crowding the other side of the board and squabbling about which piece to move".[14] The European states ended up having no real political engagement strategy. More surprising, they could not even come together on a common economic approach to China – even as the EU's trade deficit with China reached €170 billion.

A *realpolitik* Chinese scholar, Pan Wei, was to write in 2008: "The EU is weak, politically divided and military non-influential. Economically, it's a giant, but we no longer fear it because we know that the EU needs China more than China needs the EU." While probably an extreme view, Pan's comments were partially reflected in the official view. Angered over European human rights condemnations and concluding the EU would not defy the US over its arms embargo, "China downgraded its political expectations of Europe at the very moment when it upgraded its relationship with the United States."[15] The European sovereign debt crisis only accentuated a Chinese sense that the EU, far from representing a superior political and economic system, was at best an equal to the Chinese model. As Fu Ying, China's Vice-Minister of Foreign Affairs, told a German journalist who quizzed her about Western concerns regarding China's intentions, "Get down off your high horse of being on top of the world. Come down to be equals and join us on a level playing field."[16]

No surprises that the EU, having spent so much time talking to China about how they could cooperate in building a multipolar world that would contain US power, began changing its tune. When the present US Ambassador to the EU, William Kennard, presented his credentials to the President of the European Commission, Jose Manuel Barroso, in 2010 the latter talked of the "potential power of the US-EU partnership to challenge China's role in the developing world, in particular through regulatory convergence".[17]

The European Union and India

The Chinese example raises another question. Why has the EU-India relationship proved such barren ground? The assumption is that India, a democracy with a vibrant civil society, would be a more natural partner for a postmodern political structure like today's Europe. Yet, this has not proved to be the case.

There are two obvious reasons why this has not been a priority. One, has been the lack of an economic underpinning comparable to that which exists between the EU and China. The EU is India's largest trading and investment partner, but still on a scale about one-tenth that of China.

Two, India was for a long time treated by continental Europeans as the diplomatic property of the United Kingdom. "We have deferred to London when it comes to your country," said a German diplomat to me several years ago. They have thus been blinded to the thinning of the Anglo-Indian relationship over the past few decades, a dilution in large part because of the displacement of Commonwealth ties by Britain's strengthening identification with Europe.[18] Some of the reasons for neglect are eccentric. French scholars designated India a member of the "Anglosphere" – a linguistic breakup of the world quite foreign to Indian thinking. They have been surprised, when they dig a bit deeper, they find no Indian interest in the idea.[19]

Third, there is far less role for soft power exertion by Brussels in a relatively open society like India. Individual European governments, like the Netherlands, are among the largest foreign funders of nongovernmental organizations in India. Indian civil society engagement with its European counterparts is considerable – but outside the realm of government-to-government relations. Nonetheless, there are gaping holes in civil society interaction between Europe and India, most notably the lack of a large Indian diaspora in any of the major continental European nations.[20] This has been a crucial element in the development of Indo-US relations, for example, including building technological and service economy linkages.

Finally, but one that I think lies at the heart of the failure of the two countries to find any strategic depth in their relations, are the two contrasting views of sovereignty. Among all the emerging economies, India is arguably the most sensitive about the issue of sovereignty. Even when compared to China, a country imbued with a similar sense of nationalism, India is far more averse to the idea of surrendering sovereign power to multilateral or even bilateral understandings.

In a study based on interviews of the strategic elites of India and China, Rollie Lal found that her Indian responders were singularly focussed on the need for their country to maintain the sovereignty of decision-making in the international arena. So much so that even the purpose of developing military capability was less about security than about providing leverage to maintain that sovereignty. Chinese respondents, on the other hand, saw the territorial integrity of their country and the maintenance of domestic stability as being their priorities. These were issues that barely figured on the Indian radar, so confident were Indians of their democratic polity and institutions. As a result, for example, Beijing was far more open to foreign investment on its soil as it saw this as an economic fillip to maintaining domestic order. India, on the other hand, saw foreign investment partly through a prism of sovereignty.[21]

Three of the five major EU foreign policy priorities – the advancement of human rights, prevention of violent conflict and the promotion of good and democratic governance – are areas that are deep in Indian sovereignty minefields.[22] This is particularly true because, in the area of government-to-government relations, the obvious issue which combines all three in South Asia is Kashmir – a policy concern that brings out the worst in Indian touchiness. Unfortunately, the EU's postmodern interests and limited hard power in Asia have made it difficult to find a strategic area beyond these specific issues. India does not expect Europe to contribute much to its perpetual migraine of Pakistan. It assumes the EU cannot even dream of standing up to China, given Brussels' track record on that front. India, as Henry Kissinger once said, lives in a tough neighbourhood and postmodern ways and means tend to have little use in such environments. Indians assume a lack of strategic convergence with Brussels.[23]

Unsurprisingly, India has preferred to have the US as its primary interlocutor in the West for almost all its foreign policy concerns. Not only is the US a major power in the Asia, with a presence in both the Indian and Pacific Ocean regions, it thinks in a manner much closer to that of a modern state – a paradigm that Indian officials are more at ease with. One should add that the US has been on a learning curve on how to handle India that Europe has only begun to move along. A 2009 interaction between the EU and US on South and Central Asia is revealing. The State Department official repeatedly asked how India could be persuaded to be a more active player in the region, noting that the "US was interested in new ideas on how we could work with the EU to engage India." He also said "the US felt that India was also ready to play a larger and more collaborative role in international organizations. . . and in the region." The US wanted a "dialogue" with India on Burma and saw India as "absolutely critical" when it came to Afghanistan-Pakistan. The EU official seems to have had little to say on India. He offered no ideas about how to engage India. He felt China had been more constructive on Burma than India. His only response was to raise the Kashmir issue – and to be told by the US side that "it was publicly off the table".[24] In recent times, India has not only found itself on the opposite side of the EU on a number of multilateral initiatives including airline emissions and a financial transaction tax, it has taken on the task of lobbying hard against them in the international arena. The sense that the EU, despite its supposed comfort with multilateralism, is developing a taste for imposing unilateral sanctions on the rest of the world is going down poorly with the Indian establishment.[25] The new EU "Foreign Minister" Catherine Ashton has sought to engage India more closely, but being taken seriously by the Indian side in anything other than trade issues continues to be a problem. This is not specific to the EU. It is no accident India has had equally poor strategic content in its relations with other postmodern states like Canada, Australia and Japan. And if its relations are improving with the latter two, it is in large part because the rise of China is forcing Australia and Japan to relook at the world as a place where force and military might still matter.

The EU and Asian Regionalism

The quandary of the European model, and its radical postmodern security assumptions, is only underlined when one looks at the issue of Asian regional architecture. The Association of Southeast Asian Nations (ASEAN), and its expanding *avatar*, the East Asia Summit (now Plus Three) is the most successful example of Asian multilateralism. It tends to fare poorly when measured against the EU because while it is now huge – with the Plus Three it encompasses a third of the world's population – it has limited depth. But ASEAN is not, never has been and is unlikely in the foreseeable future to be a postmodern structure. It clearly sees itself as an attempt to regulate a nation-state system, not replace it with something supranational or even transnational.

This distinction is important. The United Nations, it should be pointed out, has a Charter that reflects a modern system. It sees the nation-state as the building block of the international system – the veto power is a deference to the existence of great powers. It merely tries to regulate the actions between nation-states and legitimize the idea of collective action among its members. The EU, on the other hand, seeks to dissolve the functions of the nation-state. It may not be trying to form a supranational entity as much as a transnational one. But it differs from the UN system and most existing multilateral organizations in its rejection of nation-state sovereignty and insistence on security by ending the distinction between foreign and domestic.

ASEAN is not merely cut from the same cloth as the UN, it insists on making that clear in its own pronouncements and actions. The so-called "ASEAN way", a reference to the loose normative ways that govern the organisation's consultative process, stresses "non-interference and "respect for the core issue of sovereignty".[26] Both which of could not be more antithetical to the European model. Forced attempts to compare the two organizations read like tales of ships passing by in the night. Asian regionalism has had weak, elite and largely economic interests as its drivers from the start. Nothing coming even close to the historical catacalysms that propelled European unity has occurred in the countries of Southeast Asia.[27]

Even the analytical frameworks differ. Asian regionalism focuses on inclusively bringing in as more and more nations with a glue of economics and security consultations. European concerns about structures and values barely exist. As one analysis of such literature points out: "Asian policymakers and many scholars tend not to examine formal institutions, while

EU specialists regard them as an essential and necessary foundation for the integrative process."[28]

This is hardly to say Asian regionalism is a success. Its limitations were made obvious during the Asian exchange rate crisis of 1997-1998 when its weak regional architecture failed to even coordinate policies and left most Asian countries to devise unilateral nation-specific solutions to the crisis. The far bigger challenge lies in the foreign policy and security sphere. The East Asian Summit structure is struggling to hold a rising China in place. Even the ASEAN system is struggling to ensure a more ambitious Indonesia does not force the association's ambit to be restricted forever to only trade and investment policy.

Asian regionalism, in other words, is a tale whose plot is more akin to that of the Kellogg-Briand Pact or the Concert of Europe than the EU. In the future, of course, the EU may well prove to be the model. But Asia will have many more hoops to jump through before it reaches that degree of confidence, integration and post-sovereignty. And the EU will need to iron out a lot of its own wrinkles before it can expect to set an example.

The EU and Asia's Future

The present European sovereign debt crisis will not be, in my view, fatal to the Euro or monetary union. It will, however, further damage the standing of the EU model among Asians, many whom had seen the Euro as one of the tangible accomplishments of Brussels.

Ironically, even as Europe's leadership stumbles and staggers its way towards a solution of Greece's bond mountain, circumstances have given the Union a stunning opportunity to export the European model. This is the popular revolt in the Maghrib and Levant called the "Arab Spring". Here are nations in the Mediterranean backyard of Europe, places where European cultural influences are strong and whose people now seek to create representative and possible liberal polities.

Global issues like the commons of space and sea are areas where the EU has much to contribute. The EU burned its fingers badly over multilateral climate change at the Copenhagen summit, but it remains the example for the rest of the world when it comes implementing sweeping carbon emission cuts. In Australia, which recently introduced a carbon tax, the European example was cited repeatedly by the tax's supporters. Copenhagen left a residue of national climate change policies that will continue, whatever happens on the multilateral stage.

There are some other suggestions as to what the EU could do when it comes to engaging India and other Asian countries. First, the EU needs to do a better job of explaining the nature of its postmodern system. Without that understanding in place, EU policy tends to baffle most Asians who remain stuck in their more sovereign-conscious ways. Public relations in Brussels tends to be about the structure of government which only gives the impression that the postmodern vision is a Chinese puzzle made in the depths of a Kafkaesque Castle.

Second, the change in the Arab world and the renewed interest in Africa's economic and strategic potential gives Europe a chance to show its regional mettle. India, for example, has regional dialogues on Africa with a range of countries like the US and Japan. The EU has a sputtering forum with China on Africa. It is often forgotten how important Africa was to the original European unity plan: the Schuman Plan has an often forgotten line: "Europe will be able, with increased resources, to pursue the realization of one of her essential tasks, the development of the African continent."[29] Given New Delhi's ignorance of the Levant and Maghrib – as opposed to its strength of understanding of the Persian Gulf – an exchange with Europe on this front would serve both sides well.

Third, working out an accepted international legal process on military intervention would be make it easier to handle future Libyas and Syrias. As India has become more confident of its own strength and standing, it is less vociferous in its opposition to such actions. But faced with a lack of clear rules, it prefers abstentions or neutrality to support. This is not true merely for India, but for all the so-called emerging economies.

Fourth, Europe needs to push for a new kind of bilateral economic relationship that is not wholly focussed on WTO trade talks. A new relationship should focus on the private corporate sector and new entrepreneurial class of Asia. These are the beating hearts of Asia's economic rise. In India, they now eclipse the government in investment, in technological innovation, in overseas investment, in job creation – and constitute the single largest provider of taxes for the government. India's long-standing corporate ties with the UK have led the Tata Group to become the latter's largest industrial employer.[30] Similar corporate links seem to be developing between India and Germany and the Nordic countries as well. Germany is already India's second largest science and technology partner.[31]

As one recent commentator on Indian foreign policy noted: "It is in Asia that the hollowness of much European rhetoric about unity and integration is most noticeable. Asians have no particular stake in the EU's success, and feel no need to pay it unwarranted tribute."[32]

This requires Europe to regress a little from its postmodern verities. Those should be the tail of its engagement with Asia, not the entry point. Europe, the progenitor of the nation-state system, still has many strengths in that arena and many lessons to pass on to those states working their way through that paradigm. It should not shy from showing them, even if it is only to show at some latter point that it believes it has a better path.

NOTES

1 Robert Cooper, *The Breaking of Nations: Order and Chaos in the 21st Century* (London: Atlantic Books, 2003).

2 Ibid., pp. 7-12.
3 Jean Monnet, *Memoirs* (New York: Doubleday, 1978), p. 7.
4 Cooper, n. 1, p. 30.
5 Charles Grant, "Europe Must Build a Strategic Alliance with China," *Financial Times*, 9 June 2008.
6 Charles Grant, Katinka Barysch, et al., *Embracing the Dragon: The EU's Partnership with China* (London: Centre for European Reform, 2005), p. 7.
7 Ibid., p. 52.
8 David Shambaugh, "China and Europe: The Emerging Axis," *Current History*, September 2004, pp. 243-248. "We need China to want what we want," said one EU diplomat. John Fox and Francois Godement, *A Power Audit of EU-China Relations* (London: European Council for Foreign Relations, April 2009), p. 1.
9 Grant and Barysch, n. 6, p. 21.
10 China, Ministry of Foreign Affairs, "China's EU Policy Paper, 13 October 2002", at http://www.fmprc.gov.cn/eng/topics/ceupp/t27708.htm.
11 "Europeans View China as Biggest Threat to Global Security," *Der Spiegel*, 15 April 2008. http://www.spiegel.de/international/world/0, 1518, 547492, 00.html)
12 Wikileaks document. http://www.cablegatesearch.net/cable.php?id=09BRUSSELS1656&q=barroso%20kennard.
13 Fox and Godement, n. 8, p. 1.
14 Ibid., p. 3.
15 Francois Godemont and Jonas Parello-Plesner, "The Scramble for Europe," *Policy Brief ECFR/37*, July 2011. http://www.ecfr.eu/content/entry/chinas_scramble_for_europe, p. 2.
16 "The West has become very Conceited," *Der Spiegel*, 22 August 2011, http://www.spiegel.de/international/world/0, 1518, 781597-3, 00.html.
17 Wikileaks document, http://www.cablegatesearch.net/cable.php?id=10BRUSSELS42&q=barroso%20kennard.
18 Pramit Pal Chaudhuri, "Corporate Britain has a Blind Spot About India...," *Parliamentary Brief*, September 2010. http://www.parliamentarybrief.com/2010/09/corporate-britain-has-a-blind-spot-about-india-and-it.
19 Karine Lisbonne de Vergeron, *Contemporary Indian Views of Europe* (London: Chatham House, 2006).
20 The Indian population in the largest continental European country, Germany, is 35,000. See figures in the Report of the High Level

Committee on the Indian Diaspora, Indian Ministry of External Affairs at http://indiandiaspora.nic.in/diasporapdf/chapter11.pdf.

21 Rollie Lal, *Understanding China and India: Security Implications for the United States and the World* (Westport, CT: Praeger Security International, 2006).

22 Karen Smith, *European Union Foreign Policy in a Changing World* (Cambridge: Polity, 2008).

23 Lisbonne de Vergeron, n. 19.

24 Wikileaks document. http://www.cablegatesearch.net/search.php?q=Moran+Curtin+South+Asia&qo=0&qc=0&qto=2010-02-28.

25 See for example, "India to Lead Campaign against EU Carbon Levy, Mint, 22 September 2011, http://www.livemint.com/2011/09/21235903/India-to-lead-campaign-against.html; "Europe may act alone on Financial Transactions Tax," *Der Spiegel*, 31 October 2011 at http://www.spiegel.de/international/europe/0,1518,794954, 00.html; and Prime Minister Manmohan Singh's statement at the G-20 Cannes Summit criticizing the financial transactions tax, 3 November 2011, arguing that in a country where a large portion of the financial sector remains state-owned such a tax this would make little sense as "equity holders and taxpayers are mostly one and the same" and would only serve to increase the cost of capital. See http://www.mea.gov.in/mystart.php?id=530118483).

26 Philomena Murray, "East Asian Regionalism and EU Studies," *Journal of European Integration*, 32(6), November 2010, pp. 597-616, and Amitav Acharya, *Whose Ideas Matter?: Agency and Power in Asian Regionalism* (Ithaca: Cornell University Press, 2009).

27 Acharya, n. 26.

28 Murray, n. 26; see also Peter Katzenstein and Takashi Shiraishi, *Beyond Japan: The Dynamics of East Asian Regionalism* (Ithaca: Cornell University Press, 2006).

29 Monnet, n. 3, p. 10.

30 "Tata for Now," *The Economist*, 10 September 2011.

31 B.M. Gupta and Prem Gupta, "Analysis of India's S&T Research Capabilities and International Collaborative Strength, particularly in context of Indo-German Collaboration 2004-09," DFG India, 2011, http://www.dfg.de/download/pdf/dfg_im_profil/geschaeftsstelle/dfg_praesenz_ausland/indien/111103_dfg_nistads_report.pdf).

32 David Malone, *Does the Elephant Dance? Contemporary Indian Foreign Policy* (Oxford: Oxford University Press, 2011), p. 283.

2

India and the European Union: Common Quest for Multilateralism and a Multipolar World Order

B. Krishnamoorthy

India – the largest democracy – and the European Union – the largest union of democracies – are two prominent global actors in present-day international politics. Their greatest strength is unity in diversity and pluralism which bring them closer.[1] India was the first among the non-Community member countries which had developed a close and regular official relationship with the European Community since the early 1960s and was offered a preferential treatment by the Community in its economic relations. This situation continues to be the case, though with certain occasional hiccups.

This chapter attempts to examine the approaches of India and the EU towards multilateralism and a multipolar world order. It seeks to critically analyse and evaluate European efforts in this connection and assesses their reservations about the Indian commitment to the cause of multilateralism. It also discusses the Indian espousal of multilateralism and a multipolar world order.

Multilateralism and Multipolarity

The term "multipolarity" refers to the presence of multiple power centres which seek to play an influential role in international politics, thereby making it multilateral, rather than unilateral and dominated by a single power. To Álvaro de Vasconcelos, "multipolarity" denotes the emergence of a plurality of global actors, which limit the power of the US superpower and that of other 'poles' such as the EU. He also refers to the rise of China and India, to the resurgence of Russia and to the growing importance of players like Brazil, particularly in the world economy. While distinguishing multipolarity and multilateralism, de Vasconcelos points out:

> The first is an expresssion of the way power is distributed at world level, the second an expression of how that reality should be acted upon, in other words of how that power should be used and to what ends. Multipolarity heralds a more complex international system, consistent with today's international distribution of power and the way it is both maximised and constrained by global interdependence.[2]

India and Multilateralism

As a matter of both policy and strategy, India has long staked its influence in international politics heavily on multilateral institutions – the Commonwealth, the Non-Aligned Movement, the United Nations and, to a limited extent, the World Trade Organisation. It is an active participant in the UN system and UN peacekeeping missions. In all these fora, India projects itself as the leader of the less privileged and systematically exploited developing world. India has also tended to position itself somewhere between the powerful and the powerless, the rich and the poor as well as between contending/clashing ideological groups. It adopted a policy of non-alignment in order to achieve national autonomy in foreign policy formulation and practice.[3]

While in the December 2004 poll, 55 per cent of Indians maintained that the influence of the United Nations would be mainly positive and 23 per cent felt that it would be mainly negative, in the poll of November 2005, about 44 per cent of Indians considered that the UN's influence would be mainly positive, while 12 per cent still felt that it would be basically negative. A majority of Indians felt that it would be a mainly positive change if the UN became significantly more powerful in world affairs. An overwhelming majority of Indians (88 per cent) supported the inclusion of India as a permanent member of the UN Security Council, while just one per cent did not concur.[4]

India and a Multipolar World Order

Indians prefer a multipolar world order to a unipolar one. In a 2005 GlobeScan poll, Indians were divided when asked whether Europe was becoming more influential than the United States in world affairs: 35 per cent were mostly positive while 38 per cent were mostly negative.[5] However, most Indians did not want the United States to continue to be the sole military superpower in the world either. When asked in the Pew poll (2006) if it would be better if Europe (China or another country for that matter) became as powerful as the United States, 81 per cent of the Indians said yes. Only 15 per cent Indians wanted the United States to remain the sole military superpower.[6]

In early 2005, Arvind Virmani, former Director of the Indian Council for Research on International Economic Relations (ICRIER), New Delhi, maintained that the world was rapidly becoming a tri-polar world with the United States, China and India as three power centres. While analyzing the possibility of the EU becoming the fourth pole in a quadri-polar world, he maintained that it could happen provided the EU-4 (France, Germany, Italy and the UK) allowed their individual global power to be completely eclipsed by that of the Union or if soft power counted more than military power in the twenty-first century.[7] Since this was unlikely, Virmani concluded that the European Union was neither a contender for multipolarity nor a likely pole in an emerging multipolar world because of demographic decline and because the EU is not "a virtual State"[8] with Member States, especially the larger ones, unlikely to accept any reduction of their national power in the foreseeable future.[9]

European Design for a Multipolar World

With the end of the Cold War, the European leaders maintained that unipolarity and American unilateralism would not prove beneficial even for Americans and advocated a new and just multipolar world order.[10] For instance, French Foreign Minister Hubert Védrine advocated the formation of a multipolar world. "A strong and united Europe" as well as Russia, China, Japan and India were viewed as prospective poles of an emerging multipolar world order. He urged India to join French efforts in designing "cooperative multi-polarity" with an improved version of multilateralism that respects all members of the international community as expressed by the United Nations.[11]

European analysts like Dominique Moisi argue that the world is reverting to its pre-war multipolar state – "asymmetrical multi-polarity"[12] – despite America's objective military superiority over all others. Moisi maintained that this reflected a tectonic shift in the international system: a shift from a unipolar to a multipolar world. America's unipolar 'moment', which began in 1991 with the collapse of the Soviet empire, he remarked, was over and it was no more an unipolar 'era' as claimed by Charles Krauthammer.[13] Moisi conceded that the United States was more than a "normal power", but he added that "America no longer qualifies, if it ever did, as a 'hyper power', to use Védrine's term, though it is still far from being a 'normal' power".[14]

EU, a Votary of Multilateralism

In the post-Cold War era, Secretary of State Madeline Albright asserted that the United States should pursue "assertive multilateralism", by increasing its reliance on international institutions, rules and patnerships. However, enormous confidence over the American destiny and difficulties during the UN-mandated intervention in Somalia and the Bosnia debacle, prompted UN-bashing and criticism of the EU by the Americans.[15] The EU's 'effective multilateralism' is a response to the neo-Conservatives' military unilateralism since the Europeans sincerely believed that the UN provided the legitimacy and the capacity to deal with international security and other global issues.[16]

The EU is instinctively oriented towards a multilateral approach since the Union itself is the process as well as the product of multilateralism. The entire history of European integration, in fact, can be regarded as a patient yet consistent attempt to rebuild intra-European relations on the basis of rules and regulations, a system of laws, and decision-making procedures. The Union, in fact, is an outstanding example of institutionalized multilateralism, of the sharing of sovereignty for common goals. It is, therefore, natural for the Union to preach and practice multilateralism in its domestic and foreign affairs.[17] Modeled on the principle of 'unity within diversity', it is quite natural for the Union to envisage international relations in a similar way and to champion global governance and international politico-economic relations. This reflects the Union's initiative and active role in the World Trade Organization, the Kyoto Protocol, and the establishment of the International Criminal Court. The EU represents the most advanced form of multilateralism and its experience equips it with a global reach because of its inherent nature, its relative success in promoting its collective interests in the development of an international system based on norms and rules. Otherwise, in a system based on power politics, the EU could not aspire for anything more than a complementary and secondary role to that of the United States.[18]

The Europeans argue that they approach and handle problems with greater nuance and sophistication and seek to influence others through subtlety and indirection. They claim that they are more tolerant of failure and more patient when solutions are not instantly forthcoming. Their preference is for peaceful responses to problems, through negotiation, diplomacy and persuasion instead of coercion and sabre-rattling. They advocate reliance on international law, international conventions, and international opinion to adjudicate disputes. They try to use 'soft power' like commercial and economic ties to influence third countries. The Europeans tend to often emphasize process over result, believing that ultimately process can become substance.

The Europeans contend that their postwar experience is something worth emulating by third countries. As European Commission President Romano Prodi remarked:

> The genius of the founding fathers lay in translating extremely high political ambitions . . . into a series of more specific, almost technical decisions. This indirect approach made further action possible. Rapprochement took place gradually. From confrontation we moved to willingness to cooperate in the economic sphere and then on to integration.[19]

This historical lesson borne out of their experience is what many Europeans believe they have to offer the world: not power, not its 'raw' use, but the transcendence of power. The "essence" of the European Union is essentially all about subjecting inter-state relations to the rule of law. Europe's experience of successful multilateral governance has, in turn, produced an ambition to convert the world and to recreate it on its image. Europe, Prodi adds, has "a role", "a mission" to play in global governance – a role based on replicating the European experience on a global scale. In Europe, "the rule of law has replaced the crude interplay of power... power politics have lost their influence" and by "making a success of integration we are demonstrating to the world that it is possible to create a method for peace". The transmission of the European miracle to the rest of the world has, therefore, become Europe's new *mission civilisatrice* (civilizing mission).

The European Union is not merely a votary of 'multilateralism', but advocates an increased role of the United Nations, and insists on the need for international laws, agreements, rules and institutions, which can implement and police them. It sincerely believes that breaches of universally accepted norms must not be allowed to go unpunished and governance schemes have to be gradually freed from the recurring veto-paralysis that made them largely ineffective throughout the Cold War era. The Union's primary goal is to promote global and regional governance and 'effective multilateralism'. Multilateralism, it feels, must empower the international community to resolutely deal with major global and regional issues. Effective multilateralism, in fact, is a system designed to enable the states that form the international community to act in unison to tackle common challenges and resolve problems. It should not become an instrument seeking mutual containment and result in inaction and paralysis. The EU, as the *European Security Strategy* (December 2003) points out, envisages that "international organisations, regimes and treaties to be effective in confronting threats to international peace and security, and must therefore be ready to act when their rules are broken".[20] It is but natural for Europeans to emphasize the need to ensure that the United Nations and other institutions of global governance should operate as effectively as possible and on multilateral cooperation. As Chris Patten, former European Commissioner in charge of External Relations, asserted: "The main role of the EU in international affairs must be to give teeth and bite to this multilateralism."[21] While elaborating the relations between the EU and the UN, Espen Barth Eide maintains: "The EU needs the UN and the UN needs the EU. For the EU, the UN is both the main partner and the main arena for fostering better global governance".[22]

The lack of overall strategic direction, which remained an impediment to the EU actorness earlier, as Bretherton and Vogler point out, was remedied by the *European Security Strategy*, which outlined key global challenges and key threats. Three 'strategic objectives', viz. addressing key threats, promoting security in the Union's 'neighbourhood' and supporting 'an international order based on effective multilateralism, were identified by High Representative for CFSP Javier Solana, thus marking a clear cut direction for the EU to follow.[23] This European emphasis on developing "well functioning international institutions and a rule-based international order" was generally considered to be the most important difference when compared to American foreign policy. In fact, it reflected the Union's active role in promoting international organizations and treaties.[24]

Solana identified two strategies to deal with these threats: "We need to pursue our objectives both through multilateral cooperation in international organisations and through partnerships with key actors and to develop strategic partnerships with the US, Russia, Japan, China, Canada and India."[25] The *European Security Strategy* identified the UN Charter as the "fundamental framework" for international relations and urged that it be strengthened on a priority basis.[26] Under the framework of the European Security and Defence Policy, the Union has developed operational capacity to undertake peacekeeping and conflict prevention missions outside the Union in accordance with the principles of the UN Charter. In short, the European effort seeks to embed its efforts in overall multilateral strategies, ideally to be led by the United Nations, since they are convinced that all contemporary challenges that the world confronts requires multilateral action to be decided in multilateral fora.

"Effective multilateralism" has therefore become the trademark of the European Union. The Union is fully committed to maintaining and developing international law and the UN system. Brussels asserts that international legitimacy must underpin any action undertaken by the international community in response to the global challenges. This motivates the EU to maintain a leading role of the UN in climate change and to continue to strengthen the WTO in their effort to bring about fair rules for international trade. Foreign policy, de Vascancelos argues, can only be successful if it contributes to the "multilateralisation of multipolarity" and forges strategic partnerships with regions or countries that the EU identifies as the most suited to deal with current global problems like humanising globalisation so that it may be beneficial to every one.[27]

In recent years, EU Member States have been relatively successful in coordinating their positions in the UN General Assembly and related UN bodies. The fact that the EU can muster 27 votes from Member States and enlist the votes of candidate countries and associates has transformed the Union into a power to be reckoned with within the UN system. However, in the UN Security Council, where decisions are taken on key issues of international security, the Union is not present. However, since 1993 the practice of presenting written and verbal statements on behalf of the EU has developed, with both the Presidency and CFSP High Representative Javier Solana regularly addressing the Security Council.[28]

Common Quest for Multilateralism and a Multipolar World

India and the European Union have been having annual summits since June 2000 encompassing discussion on wide-ranging issues of common concern such as international terrorism, having interlinks with drug trafficking, posing a major threat to regional and international peace and security. The declaration issued at the inaugural summit held in Lisbon spoke of "a new strategic partnership founded on shared values and aspirations characterized by enhanced and multi-faceted cooperation". The joint declaration also recognized the need to build a coalition of interests to meet the challenges of the twenty-first century, as well as recognized the EU and India as important partners in the shaping of the emerging multipolar world.

India and the EU launched a new Strategic Partnership at The Hague in November 2004. This was based on a shared conviction in the values of democracy, fundamental freedoms (including religious), pluralism, rule of law, respect for human rights and the common preference for multilateralism in the international political architecture as the means to tackle global challenges effectively. The Communication titled "An EU-India Strategic Partnership" issued by the European Commission in this regard proposed to develop a strategic partnership with India in four key areas: *a)* cooperation in international fora on conflict prevention, the fight against terrorism and non-proliferation of Weapons of Mass Destruction; *b)* economic partnership through strategic policy and sectoral dialogues; *c)* development cooperation, and *d)* fostering intellectual and cultural exchanges. It aimed at building a viable institutional structure which could ensure more concrete deliverables. The EU also sought to intensify and broaden political dialogue. In August 2004, Indian Union responded favourably to the Communication of the European Commission and envisaged "a relationship of sovereign equality based on comparative advantage and a mutuality of interests and benefits."[29] It was hoped that such a relationship would be immune to the vicissitudes of either side's relationship with a third party.

At the New Delhi summit (7 September 2005), a Joint Action Plan (JAP) was adopted as an evolving roadmap outlining concrete actions to operationalise the partnership. The JAP addressed five global issues on which the EU and India diverged. Under the title of "Deepening Political Dialogue and Cooperation", these issues cover democracy and human rights, multilateralism, conflict prevention and post-conflict reconstruction, disarmament and non-proliferation, and terrorism. The EU-India dialogue reveals a strong identity of views on the strategic priorities and issues of vital importance to both sides. Both India and the EU advocate multilateralism in international relations and both are open to dialogue on multilateral issues such as counterterrorism, disarmament, and climate change. The largest democracies in the world share common values and beliefs that make them "natural partners as well as factors of stability in the present world order".[30] The joint statement of 30 November 2007 reiterated their determination to cooperate at the global level for the cause of peace, security and sustainable development.[31] Again, in the joint statement issued at New Delhi after the Tenth India-European Union Summit on 6 November 2009, both the partners not only "agreed on the importance of an effective multilateral system, centred on a strong United Nations, as a key factor in tackling global challenges" but also "recognized the need to pursue the reform of the main UN bodies, among them the General Assembly, ECOSOC and the Security Council, with a view to enhancing the representativeness, transparency and effectiveness of the system." They also "underlined the importance of successfully concluding in 2010 multilateral negotiations at the WTO for an ambitious, comprehensive and balanced agreement that fulfils the development objectives of the Round and welcomed the renewed momentum exerted by the Delhi Ministerial meeting in September 2009".[32]

Both the partners attach great importance to counter-terrorism cooperation in the framework of the United Nations. They are for the earlier finalization and signing of the Comprehensive Convention on International Terrorism under the auspices of the UN. They also share a commitment to universal ratification and full implementation of all UN counter-terrorism conventions and related protocols, as well as supporting the work of the Counter Terrorism Implementation Task Force and are committed to the implementation of the UN Global Counter-Terrorism Strategy in all its aspects.

Indians generally share the European advocacy of multilateralism as against the American tendency for unilateralism. EU Member States are keen that the United States does not give up on the UN and that rising powers such as China and India remain committed to the system. Javier Solana even warned: "In twenty years time, it will be harder to convince giants like China, India and others that a rules-based international system is in their interest too."[33] Solana's remark is the direct outcome of the European reservations about India's commitment to multilateralism. Europeans often assert that India just displays a rhetorical allegiance to multilateralism and has been skeptical towards some of the flagship EU-led initiatives including the International Criminal Court and Ottawa Convention to Ban the Use of Anti-personnel Landmines.

Europeans maintain that India aspires to be a Great Power, sides with the US and tries to take benefit of its new found closeness with the sole super power on many issues. For instance, de Vasconcelos maintains that "newer and aspiring world powers like India have a different conception of multilateralism from that of the EU, closer to the containment of the more powerful states and the assertion of their own sovereignty than to playing their part in building an effective multilatral system". Again, he asserts that India's "strong sovereignty" posture leads to a natural tendency to favour bilateralism and a much more conservative view of multilateralism.[34]

Europeans were apparently shocked when the 2005 Pew Global Attitudes Poll showed that the share of Indians expressing a positive attitude towards the US had risen from 54 per cent in 2002 to 71 per cent in 2005, a marked countertrend with respect to most other countries which took part in the poll.[35] This should not be taken as a sign of Indian apathy to multilateralism or the idea of a multipolar world and may be attributed to American willingness to accommodate

India in the nuclear field and the Europeans failure to do so. Europeans often argue that India does not acknowledge the Union as a serious political actor in the international political arena or a pole in the ensuing multipolar world order. Charles Grant laments that while many Chinese take the EU's political ambitions seriously and regard the EU as an emerging pole in a multi-polar world, most Indians do not.[36] The European grouse is that India is either unwilling to see the EU as a political equal or prepared to comprehend the complexities of the CFSP. Their grievance is that the EU is not treated at par with the US.[37] The European Press and the academic community too shares this notion of this perceived indifference on the part of all others, including the Indians.[38] For instance, Mark Leonard and Richard Gowan argue that the EU's obsession with legality is generally taken "as a terminal sign of weakness".[39]

Reacting to Virmani's report of an emerging tripolar world mentioned earlier, Laïdi maintains that

> the Indians stick to an extremely classic vision of sovereignty and power, and with regard to Europe its entire dynamic is seen from the angle of a zero-sum game between member states and the Union. The question of sovereignty in fact rebounds on all aspects of Euro-Indian relations in that the Indians cannot help but be wary of a European project that seeks to erode the sovereignty of its members – and thus its partners – whereas India is striving by all possible means to enhance its power as a nation. For the Indians, for instance, the notion of 'shared sovereignty' is simply synonymous with 'intergovernmental cooperation'.

He attributes the lesser Indian appreciation of the EU and its accomplishments to latter's skewed perception on sovereignty and power. Laidi concludes that powers like India seek to construct a multipolar order, not necessarily a multilateral world in order to acquire a privileged status that will enable them to negotiate on an equal footing with the United States. For them,

> Europe will always appear as a power that is both more attractive and less convincing. More attractive because, not being a hard power, it

> seems a more reasonable power, more sensitive to other people's arguments, more willing to compromise than to enter into confrontation. But at the same time, it will prove to be less convincing, and even less credible, precisely because it is not a coercive power.[40]

Indian efforts to move closer to the US are regarded by European analysts as an attempt to enhance its status and say in the international politics in the company of the United States. On many issues, New Delhi prefers bilateralism in dealing with EU Member States bypassing the EU as a collectivity. Many European analysts contend that India believes that its new strategic partnership with the United States can make a difference in its quest for playing a greater role in world politics.[41]

Unfortunately, the vicissitudes of the EU experiment and the on-and-off nature of the India-EU relations have adversely influenced the India's political leadership as well as top bureaucracy. In November 2002, Foreign Minister Yashwant Sinha stated that the European Union will "perhaps be a counter balance and force in the international global situation" when it can have a "convergence of views on economic, political and strategic matters which are globally important".[42] Former Foreign Secretary Shashank expressed his misgivings about the CFSP postures of the Union. He asserted that though the Europeans realized the problems and issues of concern to India, they have not been able to find "sufficient flexibility" in decision-making owing to requirements of wide-ranging consultations.[43]

This negative attitude also prevails amongst a section of the academic community as well. EU Member States, Radha Kumar argues, are diplomatically more active within India than the Union and until some sort of a balance is achieved between the two in the context of Europe's external relations, the EU will be perceived as "a funding and trading organization than as a strategic policy-maker".[44] C. Raja Mohan, a well-known critic of the EU, asserts that the Union's self-perception of its postmodern orientation actually reflects the fact that the Continent no longer faces external and internal threats to its security. This essentially offers a convenient escape from confronting emerging challenges.[45] He justifies the "American bias" amongst Indians since the United States had recently been willing "to undertake political risks" in dealing with India whereas Europe has not been willing to do so. He is skeptical about the whole concept and process of CFSP. "The so-called CFSP," he argues, "is extremely elusive when 15 member states are going to draw a statement. Try and imagine 27 member states seeking to do it."[46] Indian scholars conclude that the EU's failure to achieve a coherent CFSP has made a substantive policy partnership with India unlikely.

Scholars like Rajendra Jain maintain that the EU seems to be a "status quoist" power whereas the United States is open to changes in the international system because of changing realities as illustrated by the Indo-US nuclear deal (July 2005). The Union, on the other hand, has retained its traditional stand on the Non-Proliferation Treaty in spite of its realization/ appreciation of the Indian quest for nuclear energy. Jain argues that India confronts traditional security threats and therefore cannot rely on soft power advocated by the EU.

> Postmodernist Europe is increasingly becoming a norms entrepreneur and exporter with somewhat of a missionary attitude seeking to reflexively impose European social, economic and ideological standards of behavior and norms within the international community through institutions in such as way as the application of these norms is considered necessary for global governance. This is to be done on the basis of the principle of sovereignty-sharing in the management of global public goods and issues like human rights, environment protection, etc.

The Europeans have come to believe that their transcendence of power holds lessons for others, and they have "a civilizing mission" in the modern and pre-modern states irrespective of their stage of development.[47] Radha Kumar too asserts that the EU is essentially a status quo power in its relationship with India whereas the United States tends to be a revisionist power, ready to rewrite the rules of the game in favour of India.[48]

Indian scholars therefore tend to believe that there is an in-built incompatibility between the India and the European Union because there is a gap between how Europeans preach and practice multilateralism, which runs counter to the Indian national security interests. They also note with utmost dismay that the Union has no policy on the issues they care most about. These include India's bid for a permanent seat in the UN Security Council with veto power and its efforts to lift the sanctions imposed by the Nuclear Suppliers Group after India's atomic tests in 1998.[49] The European criticism of India that it aspires to achieve its national interests in the name of multilateralism is also true of the EU as well. As de Vasconcelos remarks, "to have its say in world politics the EU needs to work within a system governed by rules and norms. It needs a world governed by an encompassing and effective multilateral system if it is to exert its influence".[50] Europeans should not be critical of India, but try to understand and appreciate the latter's compulsions and perspectives.

Conclusion

To the EU, effective multilateralism implies that military power can be used under certain circumstances to deal with challenges to international peace and security, but only under authorization by the United Nations. To that end, the Union seeks to cooperate with regional organizations and emerging powers like India. According to de Vasconcelos, democracy, traditional leadership of the non-aligned movement, the enduring influence of Gandhi's non-violent tradition, and the popularity of human security doctrines, which are the hallmarks of India, are more compatible with the EU's multilateral perspective.[51]

John Humphrey and Dirk Messner predict that by 2025–2030, the United States, China, India and possibly Europe will constitute four substantial poles of power in the architecture of global governance and the future interplay among these central actors of global governance will largely determine whether and how the transboundary and global problems of the twenty-first century are dealt with and what role the world's developing regions will be able to play in world politics and economics. Again, they caution that the future will be shaped by "turbulent multilateralism".[52]

The EU is considered as a force for peace, human rights, diplomacy and multilateralism due to its unique political indentity and its global impact and this factor makes the Union fit to be labeled as an 'international public good'. The EU as an emerging power will facilitate the creation of a multipolar world. However, the Union's role as a major world player is contingent on its ability to shape a world order based on a new multilateralism. The biggest challenge that the Union confronts in this regard is to reconcile the emerging multipolar international system with a sustainable and effective multilateral order in which newer and aspiring great powers like India can assume a befitting international role as well as responsibilities. Brussels has to fine-tune so as to have a balanced relationship with both New Delhi and Beijing.

Thus, both India and the EU regard themselves as votaries of multilateralism, but this tends to be self-centred. This partly explains why public opinion in the two entities has negative perceptions of each other. This may often be also due to misunderstanding, misinformation and mismanagement of their respective affairs. Instead of expressing reservations about India's commitment to multilateralism, the Union should try to accommodate Indian views and interests. Both India and the EU should cooperate in make the multilateralism a workable option and the multipolar world order a reality.

NOTES

1 "Relations between India and EU have grown from strength to strength." (7 November 2004) On the eve of the India-EU Summit at the Hague, Dutch Ambassador in India Eric F. Ch. Niehe spoke about India-EU relations to Dipanjan Roy Chaudhury. http://www.icfdc.com/html/newsarchives/external/_relations_between_india_and_eu.html.

2 Álvaro de Vasconcelos, " 'Multilateralising' Multipolarity," in Giovanni and Alvaro de Vasconcelos, eds., *Partnerships for Effective Multilateralism – EU Relations with Brazil, China, India and Russia,* Chaillot Paper, no. 109, May 2008, pp. 13 and 22.

3 Sunil Khilnani, "India as a Bridging Power," in Prasenjit K. Basu, et al, *India as a New Global Leader* (London: The Foreign Policy Centre, 2005), p. 8.

4 Angela Stephens, "Public Opinion in India and America," 1 March 2006, http://www.worldpublicopinion.org/pipa/articles/brasiapacificra/176.php?lb=bras&pnt=176&nid=&id= It is interesting to note that three in four Indians (77 per cent) favoured ending veto power of the permanent members of the UN Security Council when the other four permanent members support such a decision, as do 57 per cent of Americans (13 per cent of Indians and 34 per cent of Americans oppose it).

5 "23 Nation Poll: Who will Lead the World?, 6 April 2005," http://www.worldpublicopinion.org/pipa/articles/views_on_countriesregions_bt/114.php?lb=btvoc&pnt=114&nid=&id=. The poll of 23,518 people was conducted by the international polling firm GlobeScan together with the Program on International Policy Attitudes (PIPA) at the University of Maryland. The 23-nation fieldwork was coordinated by GlobeScan and completed during December 2004 in most countries. Polling was conducted by GlobeScan's network of national Research Partners from 15 November 2004 to 5 January 2005. In eight countries, the sample was limited to major metropolitan areas. The margin of error per country ranged from plus or minus 2.5 - 4 per cent. A notable feature of the poll is that Indians held a contrary view to that of the majority in the world. India was the only country not to view Europe positively, where views were evenly divided. On the other hand, 54 per cent of Indians regarded the United States as a positive influence whereas the majority in the world thought otherwise.

6 Stephens, n. 4.

7 Arvind Virmani, "A Tripolar Century: USA, China and India," *ICRIER Working Paper No. 160*, March 2005, at www.icrier.org., pp. 27-9.

8 According to Virmani, a "virtual State" is a supernational body with elements of a nation state, such as the power to tax and to use the tax revenues for security (defence and offence).

9 Arvind Virmani, Tripolar World: India, China and US, ICRIER, May18, 2005, at www.icrier.org., p. 17

10 Hubert Védrine, *Les cartes de la France a l'heure dela mondialisation* (Paris: Fayard, 2000), passim.

11 Speech delivered by Foreign Minister Hubert Vedrine at the concluding session of the seminar on "India and France in a Multi-Polar World," New Delhi, February 2000, *Strategic Digest*, 30(3), March 2000, pp. 276-7.

12 Dominique Moisi, "What went wrong with America," http://www.projectsyndicate.org/commentary/moisi7

13 Charles Krauthammer, "The Unipolar Moment," *Foreign Affairs*, 70, no. 1, 1990-91, pp. 23-33. Incidentally, Krauthammer believed that the unipolarity would not last long and assumed tht it would be in effect fr a period of about fifteen to twenty years, which is really a 'moment' in international politics. Subsequently in his article "The Unipolar Moment Revisited," *National Interest,* no. 70, Winter 2003, p. 17, Krauthammer revised his calculations and claimed: "The unipolar moment has become the unipolar era of prolonged duration."

14 Dominique Moisi, "The Fall of the Hyper Power," http://www.projectsyndicate.org/commentary/moisi12.

15 Robert Kagan, "Power and Weakness—Why the United States and Europe see the world differently," http://www.hoover.org/publications/policyreview/3460246.html; Charles Krauthammer, "An American Foreign Policy for a Unipolar World," http://www.aei.org/publications/pubID.19912, filter.all/pub_detail.asp Posted: February 12, 2004. Kagan maintains: "Europeans oppose unilateralism in part because they have no capacity for unilateralism.... For Europeans, the appeal to multilateralism and international law has a real practical payoff, with little cost." He goes on to claim that the EU is a weak power, both militarily and morally and that they are from the 'Venus', i.e. pursue a pacific policy. Krauthammer criticizes the Europeans by maintaining that "the whole point of the multilateral enterprise (of the Europeans) is to reduce American freedom of action by making it subservient to, dependent on, constricted by the will and interests of other nations and it is an attempt to tie down Gulliver with a thousand strings. It is

designed to domesticate the most undomesticated, most outsized, national interest on the planet of the Americans."

16 Vasconcelos, n. 2, p. 26.

17 http://europe.eu.int/comm/external_relationss/nfewss/patten/sp02_134.htm (14-06-02) "Developing Europe's External Policy in the Age of Globalization," speech by Commissioner for External Relations Chris Patten, 4 April 2002).

18 Vasconcelos, n. 2, pp. 18, 20

19 Speech at *Institut d'Etudes Politiques*, Paris, 29 May 2001.

20 Vasconcelos, n. 2, pp. 25-26.

21 http://europe.eu.int/comm/external_relationss/nfewss/patten/sp02_134.htm (14-06-02) "Developing Europe's External Policy in the Age of Globalization," Speech by Chris Patten, the then European Commissioner for External Relations, 4 April 2002.

22 Espen Barth Eide, "Introduction: The Role of the EU in Fostering 'Effective Multilateralism'," in Espen Barth Eide, ed., *Global Europe. Report 1: 'Effective Multilateralism': Europe, Regional Security and a Revitalised UN,* (London: Foreign Policy Centre, 2004), p. 3.

23 Charlotte Bretherton and John Vogler, *The European Union as a Global Actor* (London: Routledge, 2006), second edition, p. 218.

24 Stephan Keukeleire and Jennifer MacNaughtan, *The Foreign Policy of the European Union* (London: Palgrave Macmillan, 2008), p. 59.

25 "A Secure Europe in a Better World," European Security Strategy, Brussels, 12 December 2003, at www.consilium.europa.eu/uedocs/cmsUpload/78367.pdf.

26 Desmond Dinan, *Ever Closer Union—An Introduction to European Integration* (London: Palgrave Macmillan, 2005), p. 604.

27 Vasconcelos, n. 2, p. 30.

28 K.V. Laatikainen, "Assessing the EU as an actor at the UN: Authority, Cohesion, Recognition and Autonomy," *CFSP Forum*, 2(1), 2004, pp. 4-9.

29 "EC Communication titled "An EU-India Strategic Partnership – India's Response," 27 August 2004.

30 Ummu Salma Bava, "India-EU Relations: Building a Strategic Partnership," in Richard Balme and Brian Bridges, eds., *Europe–Asia Relations: Building Multilateralisms* (Hampshire: Palgrave Macmillan, 2008), p. 249.

31 India-EU Joint Statement, New Delhi, 30 November 2007, www.eu2007.pt/NR/rdonlyres/...0E1B.../20071130EUIndia Statement.pdf.

32 EU-India Summit, New Delhi, 6 November 2009, Joint Statement, 15582/09 (Presse 320) available at press.office@consilium.europa.eu http:/www.consilium.europa.eu/Newsroom.

33 Javier Solana, Speech to the Annual Conference of the European Union Institute for Security Studies, Paris, 25-26 September 2005.

34 Vasconcelos, n. 2, p. 27

35 Nicole Gnesotto and Giovanni Grevi, *The New Global Puzzle – What World for the EU in 2025?* (Paris: Institute for Security Studies, 2006), p. 170. However, the Europeans should not read more on the Indian attitude towards the United States at the particular juncture than warranted. It was, but natural, that President Bush and the US were darlings in the Indian eyes in the wake of the Indo-US nuclear deal, while both were unpopular in Europe because of their war with Iraq. Doubting the Indian credibility and credentials are unwarranted.

36 Charles Grant, "India and the EU: Strategic Partners?, Centre for European Reform," *CER Bulletin*, Issue 46, February/March 2006. http://www.cer.org.uk/articles/46_grant.html.

37 Peter Mandelson, "The Global Economic Agenda: Europe and India's Challenge," speech at the Confederation of Indian Industry Partnership Summit, Kolkata, 13 January 2005. EU Trade Commissioner Mandelson had publicly expressed his concern: "Just as Europe should take India seriously, I want India to take Europe seriously. Some of you may think that, if India is about the future, Europe is about the past. That would hardly be surprising given the predominance of the United States in today's world and the history of India's relationship with Europe – or at least with one European country I happen to know well. Over the years, as that old British relationship with India changed and diminished, Europe's contact with India has I feel declined. I read recently a report that Indians do not think very much about the European Union. This is a shame if it is true. For the EU is today India's largest trading partner and largest source of foreign direct investment. The European Union, like India, is also about the future."

38 Zaki Laïdi, "European Preferences and their Reception," in Zaki Laïdi, ed., *EU Foreign Policy in a Globalized World – Normative Power and Social Preferences* (London: Routledge, 2008), p. 11. Laïdi refers about indifference, which easily slides toward a certain disdain, "either because 'norms over force' hardly seems a credible stance, or because it (the EU) is perceived as 'a second-rank player' the strategic choices being made by its protectors – in this case the United States – or, finally, because Europe is only seen through its member states, each having specific

interests and practices far removed from the principles defended by Europe." He also refers to a *Le Figaro* report of 31 May 2007: "The United States are defining a crucial change of strategy for the XXIst century, which articulates on a trio composed by United States, China and India."

39 Mark Leonard and Richard Gowan, "Implementing the European Security Strategy", available at www.fpc.org.uk

40 Zaki Laidi, *Norms over Force -The Enigma of European Power* (New York: Palgrave Macmillan, 2008), pp. 11, 138.

41 Vasconcelos, n. 2, p. 23.

42 Speech by Foreign Minister Yashwant Sinha on "India's Foreign Policy: Successes, Failures and Vision in the Changing World Order," at the National Defence College, New Delhi, 18 November 2002 at http://www.meaindia.nic.in/speech/2002/11/18spc01.htm.

43 Shashank, "India and the European Union," in Rajendra K Jain, ed., *India and the European Union. Building a Strategic Partnership* (New Delhi: Radiant Publishers, 2007), p. 39.

44 Radha Kumar, "India as a Foreign Policy Actor – Normative Redux," CEPS Working Document No. 285/February 2008, p. 26, available at http://www.ceps.eu. De Vasconcelos concurs when he says: "India has tended to perceive the Union mainly as a trade actor, is quite sceptical about the EU's ability to play a relevant political and security role, particularly when it comes to Asia." De Vasconcelos, n. 2, p. 19.

45 C. Raja Mohan, *Crossing the Rubicon. The Shaping of India's New Foreign Policy* (New Delhi: Viking, 2003), pp.75-76.

46 C. Raja Mohan, "India, Europe and the United States," in Rajendra K. Jain, ed., *India and the European Union in the 21st Century* (New Delhi: Radiant Publishers, 2007), pp. 60-63.

47 Rajendra K. Jain, "European Union and Emerging Asian Powers (China and India)," paper presented at the international workshop on "European Common Foreign and Security Policy: Implications for India," Pondicherry University, 11-12 October 2010.

48 Kumar, n. 44, p. 23.

49 Grant, n. 36.

50 Vasconcelos, n. 2, p. 24.

51 Ibid., pp. 27, 30.

52 John Humphrey and Dirk Messner, "China and India as Emerging Global Governance Actors: Challenges for Developing and Developed Countries," *IDS Bulletin*, vol. 37, no. 1, January 2006, p. 108.

3

Europe and India in a Multipolar World: New Meanings of Nation, Nation-building and the Balance of Power

Hartmut Elsenhans

Europe and India have to adapt to a new international system in which they are only partially drivers of the set of norms which govern inter-state relations. They have an interest in using their bilateral relations in order to improve their positions within the set of rising new powers. Both of them are not the first choice as allies or partners for other participants in the club: Europe because of its internal divergences on the way of becoming a new type of a nation state at least in European eyes and India because of its limited capacity to be accepted as a dominant regional power in South and Southeast Asia and India's difficulty in projecting economic influence as the basis of soft power. In order to avoid being treated merely as chips in the game of others, India and Europe could develop their bilateral relationships. This is, however, constrained by the reciprocal perceptions of elites in both countries about the seriousness of the choices of the potential partner. Indians are disturbed by the proclamation of the Europeans of a new and specific character of their new policies[1] whereas the Europeans suspect India of turning back to inefficient power politics of a realistic tinge.

The central argument of this chapter consists in showing that there is no fundamental difference in approach to international relations between European and Indian decision-makers. However, there are differences in defining levels of interests following a realistic approach in foreign policies and in how foreign policies are presented and justified in order to conform to precise definitions of overall worldviews. The European civil society-oriented foreign policy "dressing" serves the purpose of creating a European identity.[2]

In a similar way, the new realist representation of Indian foreign policy behaviour reflects the end of secularism which had been promoted by an *avant garde* but which has failed in evolving from independence from colonial exploitation to social transformation and overcoming of poverty and underdevelopment.[3] The self-definition of the wretched of the earth as the new historical proletariat could no longer serve for social integration, when newly rising middle strata found all places already taken by the "brown rulers" and when an increasing number of "lumpen" lost any hope of being integrated in the state-led sector of the economy.[4] With the older secular ideals having become discredited, cultural nationalism remained the only vehicle for social integration.[5] Nationalism without the perspective of a cosmopolitan and egalitarian transformation of society could but become available as an instrument of integration of society for all those who largely justified existing hierarchies in the name of the organic unity of the nation. This required a presentation of the nation according to the realist school of international relations where the state is personified and the bearer of the national interest.[6]

European Civilizing Mission and India Emergence as a New Power

Indo-European misunderstandings are most visible in their differences in defining multilateralism as an organising principle of international political interactions. For the European Union, multilateralism means consultation under an overarching umbrella of increasingly powerful legal and civil society structures. An international civil society is expected to limit the sovereignty of the states. Sovereignty as an attribute of the state as a special actor international relations is considered as a source of oppression.[7]

For the new Indian realistic foreign policy, multilateralism means consultation for a fair compromise between admittedly very diverging interests on the basis of a balance of power. Because of this difference, both sides become frustrated, when they talk to each other on similar terms with dissimilar meanings.[8]

The Indian manifestations of these frustrations appear as a criticism of the hypocrisy of the Europeans claiming to represent an overarching general interest of mankind, with its (selective) policies of democracy promotion and human rights interventions. Europeans feel frustrated over India appears as the argument of a permanent turn of India to selfish interests similar to the nineteenth century powers in Europe, which the European integration process expressly is committed to overcome. Europe, however, claims to follow new principles, which are said to be distinct from power politics. These new principles are presented as a new step in civilising the anarchical pattern of international relations so that ultimately an international rule of law leading to more peace and more harmony can be achieved.

Such an attitude not only is based on universal norms as its supporters pretend, but supposes that these norms can be interpreted is a way where the practical implications are applying to all the participants in the international system quasi-objectively. In opposition to the supporters of such a rule-based international system, also the balance of power oriented realistic positions share in support of most of the norms. But they admit that interpretations may vary. As a result, interpretations and applications have to be negotiated.

Realism does not reject abiding to civilised norms of behaviour but opposes hegemonic positions of some members of the international community in interpreting and ultimately instrumentalizing such norms.[9]

The idea that practical requirements for behaviour can be deduced from universal norms without their being negotiated between equally respected partners appears to be preposterous to the partners of Europe in the international game. This game is characterised by the entry of previously dominated but now (so-called newly) emerging powers in the South, especially in Asia. So the European idea of developing a general set of behavioural rules out of some universally accepted norms recalls colonialism. European history in the non-European world is full of basically liberal attempts to impose itself on the rest of the world after centuries of intellectual darkness. In many countries of the South, this transformative mission of colonialism found an echo not only in the form of the bridgeheads of the colonial powers in the local societies, but especially in the form of the emergence of "modern" national movements which, after the defeat of the traditional political structures (primary resistance), became the true leaders of the process which ultimately led to independence. Significantly, some forces among the more liberal Western public interpreted the end of colonialism as a victory of the West and its political norms since the new revolutionaries of the Third World were referring to the values of the American and French revolutions.

Three salient traits of European foreign policy behaviour with respect to the South reinforce this impression. In the civil society approach, non-governmental organisations (NGOs) predominate. They are delivering services to social groups which do not dispose of the economic or political power to have access to these the same services. The political economy of NGOs is based on resource flows from such organisations to constituencies which in exchange for additional resources provide some sort of nonmaterial assets which I have called "entitlements to moral well being".[10] For the target group, there is practically no difference in cost between a large variety of such immaterial assets so that the target group is indifferent the precise contents of the immaterial assets to be delivered to the resource distributing NGO. As a result, the target group designs the immaterial assets according to the wishes of the NGOs which have very precise ideas about such assets in function of their perceptions of the motives for donating in the audience in the rich (European) publics.

NGOs in the West basically share the neoliberal economic visions of the more conservative Western constituencies for at least one basic reason.[11] They compete for their ability as representatives of the general interest not only with each other, but more even with a large block based on labour. Labour defines the overriding interest as the interest of the working people. Product differentiation implies that competitors are favoured by the choice of a competing alternative overarching concept, a non-class-based humanitarian general interest. NGOs therefore are close to the practices of Western governments and aid agencies in limiting wasteful spending in underdeveloped countries. But wasteful spending is a relative notion: Rent-based social classes, often state classes in the South,[12] are legitimate in spending on investment which is not profitable in the short term because of market failure as a characteristic trait of underdevelopment, so that other criteria than profit are important. This limits the possibility of discriminating against expenditure which others may consider as serving luxury consumption or military grandeur. A conflict over the foreign policy objectives of emerging powers with respect to military technologies is pre-programmed.

Whenever neoliberal concepts of economic governance are applied without consideration for the absence of the conditions for capitalism in marginality-ridden underdeveloped economies, strategies which take into consideration these deficiencies of market failure are considered as inefficient. As the corresponding political structures provide possibilities for particular groups with access to rents to increase their spendings, underdeveloped marginality-ridden economies are simultaneously characterised by very low levels of consumption and high prestige and luxury spending by very limited groups. This overconsumption of the few has been constantly connected to tendencies to indebtedness. The civil society-oriented approach to international relations of Europe regards in good governance a means for reducing such overconsumption.

In this context, good governance recalls the intrusion into economic affairs which regularly had been the starter of colonial takeover in the late nineteenth century. The Egyptian case of 1878, the Ottoman debt administration since 1881 together with many others (e.g. Morocco), are still in mind. Indeed, at least in sub-Saharan Africa, Western intervention since the 1980s is much more detailed than the debt administrations in the still independent countries of the late nineteenth century in the South.

Under the guise of a basically neoliberal discourse about the predominance of norms, law and order against the assertion of state power, the Europeans along with the Americans promote, an international order, where the rules tend to favour the stronger capitalist countries, admittedly with one major difference. The exports promoted this time allow the South to economically catch up. Because of the decrease of raw material rents in the wake of Western exploitation, these exports are now to the difference of the late nineteenth century no more raw materials with income and price inelastic demand, but manufactured products. Here the South has comparative advantage not only in simple labour-intensive goods, but also in new and sometimes even very sophisticated technological goods as well. This is so, because of the importance of disembodied technical progress in capitalist growth in the West. The South may be less productive than the West in high technology products, but its backwardness in productivity may be lower than in less modern, the old leading products. The profile of East Asian exports with very cheap and simple products as well as a strong position in electronic goods is an illustration.

European civil society orientation of foreign policy serves power interests of major European groups in a realistic way

Europeans have opted for a civil society-oriented foreign policy approach in their relations with South Asia in general, and with India in particular — even if in this case to a lesser degree given the power position of India on the international chessboard — basically because of Europe's limitations in translating its economic weight into political power since Europe is still under construction. Europe's foreign policies are clearly determined by its economic, financial as well as strategic and political interests in the world of the other economically developed great powers, but it is unable to pursue independent foreign policies in the rest of the world. With some exaggeration one can argue, that the links between idealistic legitimation and *realpolitik* in Europe's profile with regard to the non-North Atlantic world is mainly due to the unimportance of the policies in question. As these areas matter relatively little, foreign policies with respect to them are more easily instrumentalized than policies in other domains of external behaviour for purposes in domestic affairs. Better than other domains of foreign policy of Europe, the foreign policies directed to Africa, Asia and Latin America can inform us about the place of foreign policy in the domestic matters of the European Union, and this means in a process of nation-making, in the process of a *nation en formation*.

The objection that the treaties on the European Union had consistently excluded the idea of a European nation which would replace the old nations of the continent is not pertinent. The process of European integration has always been characterised by getting it on the track through small steps with large irreversible logics, in French, *engrenage*, where the different participating actors lose the possibility of further defending their original reluctance with respect to these unifying dynamics.

As regards the process of formation of a nation, the process of European integration must take account of two major realities: the commitment of a large part of the European elites and the reluctance of large sections of the masses.[13] This is a totally new political experiment in history. Nation-building processes had previously been characterised by processes of popular mobilisation. The French nation was the product of the resistance of popular masses against feudal exploitation. French elites had excluded the masses as plebeians of non-Frankish origin from the pre-revolution French nation. Nationalism was accepted by the ruling strata of Central and East Europe nearly uniformly only when popular unrest had become so strong that some sort of new integration had to be looked after in order to replace the failing links between feudal landlords and their serfs in their role as a glue of social cohesion.

In the case of contemporary European integration, the masses defend the nation-state because the nation-state is the locus where they can use the weight of their numbers against the more concentrated other resources of political influence at the disposal of the better-off.

The process of formation of a nation takes place in the European integration context as the probably first case where collective solidarity is created from above with respect to a threat which the masses do not yet perceive. The Indian nation was a process of mobilisation of all sectors of population against foreign domination.[14] After 1945 in Western Europe the heirs to fascist aberrations, the non-nationalists middle and upper class-based Christian Democrats launched, with the active participation especially of France, Italy, Belgium and Germany, the process of European integration in order to mobilise all their resources already now in order to preclude a later conquest by Russia in similar ways as Britain had done two centuries before in India.[15]

Foreign policies are a good area for creating symbols for such a process for a number of reasons. Economic integration as a vehicle on which unification can be based require either very heavy measures of redistribution in the case of German unification, or are characterised mainly by improving conditions for an admittedly large, but not overwhelmingly large dynamic sector of the economy, the better off. This corresponds to the largely available data on the above average support for European integration by the middle class, the young dynamic sectors and this in the regions of economic concentration of the core region stretching form Middle England to Northern Italy along the Rhine and the Western Alp Passes via the Benelux, Eastern France and most of West Germany, the so-called blue banana.

Alignment only via growth poles which attract labour from weaker areas is extremely problematic if unification is not expected to lead to perfect regional mobility of labour as had been the case in nineteenth-century German unification with massive migration of population between German regions. European social policies expressly aim at realising convergence in economic levels without massive migration. The Cardiff and Luxembourg processes aim at the promotion of skills and the empowerment of labour through fair conditions for exercising union activities, but explicitly exclude government or community level measures at harmonising wage levels.[16] Different levels in cost of manpower are seen as an instrument for allowing the catching up of technically less advanced regions as the local levels of wages will not determine overall demand for industries, so that cheap cost production sites can grow on the basis of the demand from the high manpower cost regions of the Union.

In the European integration process, harmonisation can

only be achieved by negative integration, the aligning of welfare measures by removing protective rules.[17] The European integration process cannot benefit from the traditional sources of collective action underlying state formation. European elites are therefore looking for other instruments including foreign policy, which can be conceived as contributing to a collective identity.[18] This implies that there are no conflicts between Member States of the EU over major issues in foreign policy behaviour.[19] Happily there are no major conflicts about basic orientations of the European Union with respect to overall principles of managing the world economy and the world system, especially with respect to the United States. However, conflict of interest over details have rendered a common foreign policy with respect to the main partners in the industrialised world difficult.

The only area where identity creating foreign policies can therefore be followed is in the case of the Union's relations with the South.[20] Here the real issues for the major interest groups in the European Union are limited. Because of the relative absence of the major interest groups, business and labour, other groups can have a more than usual influence, and this favours the NGOs. This fits marvellously into the preferences of the major social forces which support actively the European integration process, the middle strata of salaried workers in the blue banana area. These groups have become politically very liberal following post-materialist orientations and therefore support issues like human rights protection and safeguarding the environment, both issue areas. In order to be credible, the medicine is also applied to the larger countries of the South, with relatively limited direct and indeed decreasing success in India and China.[21]

Such preferences in foreign policy correspond also to differences in the power position of the three major member countries. Prime Minister Tony Blair has made it is clear in 1993 that there was a difference between Britain and France on the one side and Germany on the other.[22] He considered that both Britain and France had better capabilities of using openly military power. Whenever Germany succeeds in keeping the European Union from addressing issues where massive military power is required, German-French cooperation becomes easier. Wherever issues of cooperation and human rights protection are addressed, the more interest-oriented British foreign policy has less possibilities to ally with France, so that French-German cooperation becomes more likely. Germany is therefore directly interested in maintaining the civil society foreign policy orientation of the European Union in order to promote its most direct realistic power interests within the EU. In seeking to improve its relative position, Germany sees in a greater weight of European foreign policies a major instrument for achieving more international influence. Following the so-called idealism is a very practical strategy for promoting German national power interest.

With respect to traditional realist perceptions so common in Indian foreign policy thinking, it should be noted that my conclusion implies that European idealism and civil society foreign policy orientation are realist in basis, but not based on the states in their existing form as the level from which influence on the global system can be won. The North American adaptation of late nineteenth-century German realist thinking has taken too seriously the role of the existing states. It is not the state per se which defines the interests to be followed in international relations. Elite groups which have achieved the position of being entitled to directly participate in the international game, occupy the historically accidental state available to them.

The application of realist instrumentalization of civil society orientation in the Euro crisis

This pattern of using idealism and speaking about new principles in international relations for achieving power positions by means of actively promoting realist interests in exercising influence at the global level is visible in the treatment of the Euro crisis by Germany and France.

Intergovernmental cooperation for overcoming the Euro crisis is highly dependent on long-term interests as interpreted in the framework of explanations on the origins of the Euro crisis. Governments staff, including the ministers, have limited knowledge about the origins of the crisis and where some of them have, the perceived risks of following one's own analysis leads them to follow the advice of others. These others are the ones who are perceived as capable of making statements in case of failure of the type that failure was foreseeable and only the result of the governments rejecting to follow their advice. For the time being, the only group capable of such statements are the bankers themselves, those who have created the mess.

This state of affairs reflects the decade-long fight of business against dissenting views in academia as shown by the gradual disappearance of unorthodox positions in all economics faculties in EU Member States under the impulse of their business administration members and competition from rising private business administration schools for which private business applied strategies of preferential recruitment.[23] What was called New Labour was in reality the consolidation of the theoretical demise of social democracy.[24]

Banks have a veto power in explaining the situation at least as long as their solutions appear to be capable of contributing to the overcoming of the crisis. For a long while, the crisis will be explained according to the bankers' analysis as the result of overspending of irresponsible governments especially in the periphery of the European Union.

Within this framework European governments will try to limit their financial responsibilities, hence to keep their payments low, without however endangering the common currency and without expelling any Member State from the Eurozone.

Given these limitations, the following strategies will be followed:

- The highly indebted economies like Greece will be squeezed in order to maintain popular support for extracting resources from all Member States in order to pay the banks so that the argument that the European Union is not transfer community remains credible.
- Franco-German relations remain privileged so that Germany will engage itself for keeping the flow of debt service running in order to avoid disproportionate bank failures in the more exposed French banking community.
- Banks will be saved as long as possible because an alternative solution would imply a Keynesian process of destruction of fake financial capital. Such a process would indeed imply the operation of a Keynesian government at the EU level which would create Union-wide political processes as characteristic for a nation.

The Euro crisis and the rescue of the common currency will become the litmus test for all those theories which are at the basis of the European integration process, and which have promised that there might be spillovers from step to step integration measures to a new configuration within the emerging European Union. I expect that these theories will be proven as right. For this evaluation I dare to present a scenario of the further evolution of the crisis.

The proposed solutions will not work because the diagnosis is wrong. States ran into deficit in order to maintain acceptable levels of effective demand. Governments of countries with low levels of competitiveness had to resort more intensively to deficit spending than governments which were able to maintain higher degrees of competitiveness. In the discussions about the introduction of the Euro, Keynesian have constantly warned against these disequilibria.[25] The excessive use of state spending for maintaining effective demand instead of rising real incomes led to the emergence of financial assets, for which there is no counterpart in the real economy. The desire of the banks to be repaid their loans consists in nothing else than in the demand for the transformation of fake values earned in the financial markets into real values with counterparts in the real economy. This is a massive redistribution of real wealth in favour of the banks and their holders of financial assets. No economy can bear the weight of fancifully created financial assets on the basis of limited amounts of real assets, especially as capitalist economies are characterised by capital formation being limited by the amount of effective demand. Whatever the power of the banks, they will be unable to collect their loans just as the Western allies were unable after 1919 to collect the debt they imposed in the Versailles Treaty on Germany. Only the limited amount of assets of the real economy can be handed over to the holders of financial assets. This amount is limited because, in capitalism, asset formation depends ultimately on mass demand which the creditors in all such crises reduce for the purpose of paying the banks.[26]

The crisis will provoke the strengthening of European institutions. The solution of the banks will allow those governments which have to pay to monitor budgetary policies of the other governments. The actual discussions show that there can be no differential status of paying and receiving governments, but a decision making unit only at the community level, certainly largely under the influence of the paying governments. This will put into place also the mechanisms necessary for an alternative solution. It is useful that the crisis is protracted, as this gives time and space for the forces capable of proposing alternative solutions.

Unlike after crises, especially the one of the 1930s, the relations created within the European Union have already proven to be strong enough to protect the integration process from being reversed. After now more than two years, no government has openly demanded to leave the Union and no government has openly been threatened of being thrown out.

The process of destruction of fake capital implies the destruction of legally recognised claims on assets, which in capitalism occurs if the necessary destruction of capital is not realised by market competition alone.[27] One can assume that such a process of intervention into property rights will be accepted only if Union-wide coalitions emerge, as well as that the claim of a regulated, instead of a 1930-type chaotic destruction of fake financial assets will become possible only if there are large enough alliances which would support such a non-bank oriented exit from the crisis. Such Union-wide coalitions will emerge because of two inevitable and unremovable structures. The fake assets have to be destroyed just as monetary reform had to be imposed in Germany after the loss of World War II as a capitalist economy requires sound money and there is nobody who sees the crisis being solved by the transition to a centrally planned economy. Only better off economies have a real option of exit. But the richest among the better-off economies, viz. Germany, will not take this option for one simple reason: any standing alone of Germany, and especially Germany standing alone on the basis of more economic resources, will provoke a European alliance against Germany. What had failed since 1870, Germany's attempt to hegemony in Europe will certainly not be attempted by Germany now. The other possible candidate for exit, France, will certainly not be ready to hand over the remnants of the European Union to a then greatly stronger Germany. The third of the more powerful economies, Britain, will probably be tempted not to leave only the Eurozone, but the European Union when the requirements of the destruction of financial capital will hit the city of London. The option will lie between a nearby Europe Cayman Islands or Singapore with Cayman Islands being more probable.

A common argument in political science is that state power becomes more visible in periods of economic crisis. My analysis of the future trajectory of the Eurozone illustrates that the civil society-oriented approach of European foreign policy had its real results. There is no yet a European nation so far but a network of structures which enable greater integration for making more state power visible.[28] The crisis will lead to greater state power at the Union level, perhaps in the form of greater intergovernmental cooperation. This might result in the imposition of solutions on reluctant minorities.

If the crisis leads to the dissolution of the Eurozone, Germany would end up paying less, importing at cheaper prices, reducing budgetary spending and possibly enjoy rapidly rising real wages and an improvement of the terms of trade. Greece would suffer from deteriorating terms of trade but not necessarily a lower standard of living since import substitution would accelerate with declining terms of trade. That these solutions have not been chosen so far is because the definition of interests in this field of issues comprises more complex elements which incorporate other dimensions of the global and European structures. It is this greater complexity which translates into policies which seem to be more by idealistic reasons although they are only result of a balanced evaluation of a variety of interests in other fields.

The idealistic dimension realist critics of European foreign policy and European internal dynamics are so much criticising are not a reflection of a new quality of political behaviour of European elites but the result of highly realist interests in however extremely complicated situations as to be found normally in any case of a fundamental reconstruction of the social frameworks. Such processes are facilitated if they are embedded into mystiques in areas of minor interest where the creation of symbols is cheap. The human rights and civil society-oriented approach of European foreign policy serves such a purpose of creation of symbols. The defence of the Euro reflects the level to which the socially necessary state functions have already been shifted from empirically existing ethnic states and to empirically not yet fully existing structures. The point of no-return has already been passed. The crises which would have been capable of reversing this process will, under the existing conditions, only contribute to reinforce the new but yet fully operating structures in order to make them operate.

Conclusion

The conflict between European foreign policy thinking and that of India is because the latter takes the former at its face value without looking behind the facade and criticises European claims on the basis of their openly proclaimed ideological content. They do not realize the function of this proclaimed ideological content in the service of a long-term project of European elites at the European level and external dangers of the qualitative decline of Europe at the global level. Any successful process of structuring requires a myth and the EU has developed one nicely fitting into its internal limits and requirements and applicable where major European interests are not at stake.

Indian analysts have tended to focus on the instrumental and ideological character of some aspects of European foreign policy behaviour and have not sought to deconstruct European claims by bringing their instrumental character to the fore.

A similar procedure to the one presented in this chapter could consist in demonstrating that the cosmopolitan and universalist period of Indian foreign policy after Independence, under the label of non-alignment, corresponded to great power interests of India at that time which had to be abandoned not only because the structures of the international system changed, because China was no longer a rival in the rest of the Third World on the basis of ideological competition but only on the basis of give and take power politics, but because newly emerging political forces within India could not gain great internal support by presenting themselves as cosmopolitan, a profile of their internal rivals to which they responded by a greater concentration on Hindu culture.

The key to solve the *apories* presented in the metatheoretical dimensions of this chapter does not consist in opposing realism and idealism in foreign policy but to leave behind the formally existing states as the level of analysis. States serve as formal basis for politically organised groups. Such groups are imposing themselves by the use of political power. They define real interests according to the expectations of realism. These interests are sometimes considered by external observers as state interests. These groups try to impose themselves by rallying support also from those who do not share their immediate real interests. They enlarge their following by presenting their strategies as favourable to the interests and convictions of those who not share their immediate interests. Such an overlapping may really exist so that such ideologies may even constitute bases for larger coalitions. In other cases, such ideologies will simply be wrong and keep other groups from articulating their own real interests. An understanding of the embeddedness of the visible aspects of European foreign policy behaviour in an on-going process of change in Europe where complex real interests are defended and where ideological dressing is looked after in order to facilitate such change can contribute to a less passionate understanding of European foreign policies together with an insight into the real dimensions of European foreign policy behaviour. This might facilitate EU-Indian understanding and increase the possibilities for both Europe and India to avail of each other in the intensifying rivalry already engaged by more advanced powers for rank and a seat in the emerging new global system.

NOTES

1 C. Raja Mohan, *Crossing the Rubicon: The Shaping of India's New Foreign Policy* (New Delhi: Viking, 2003), p. 73; Arvind Virmani, "World Economy, Geopolitics and Global Strategy: Indo-US Relations in the 21st Century," *Economic and Political Weekly*, 41, 43-44, November 2006, pp. 4601-4612.

2 Hartmut Elsenhans, "La politique extérieure de l'Union européenne:

L'insertion de l'Europe dans un monde multipolaire en voie de formation," in Centre d'Études Européennes, ed., *Réalisations et défis de l'Union Européenne. Droit-politique-économie. Mélanges en hommage à Panayotis Soldatos* (Brussels: De Boeck, 2012), pp. 467-480.

3 Sudipta Kaviraj, "On State, Society and Discourse in India," *IDS Bulletin*, 21(4), 1990, pp. 11f.

4 Hartmut Elsenhans, "The Rise of New Cultural Identitarian Movements in Africa and Asia in the Emerging Multipolar System," *Comparative Studies of South Asia, Africa and the Middle East*, 32(3), Winter 2012, forthcoming.

5 Asef Bayat, "Activism and Social Development in the Middle East," *International Journal of Middle East Studies*, 34(1), February 2002), pp. 1f; Achin Vanaik, "The New Indian Right," *New Left Review*, 9, May/June 2001, p. 57; Deana Heath, "Communalism, Globalization, and Governmentality: Some Reflections on South Asia," *Comparative Studies of South Asia, Africa and the Middle East*, 29(3), 2009, p. 574.

6 O.P. Gupta, *Rise and Fall of Vajpayee Government* (New Delhi: Mittal, 2004), pp. 38-39. The fact is so banal to Katherina Adeney and Lawrence Sáez, *Coalition Politics and Hindu Nationalism* (London: Routledge, 2004), that it is considered as a given for the analysis, without this shift being discussed at all.

7 Klaus Scharioth, "Die neuen sicherheitspolitischen Herausford-erungen und die internationale Rolle Europas," *Integration*, 28(3), July 2005, pp. 246-250; Hazel Smith, *European Union Foreign Policy. What it is What it Does* (London: Pluto Press, 2002), p. 271; Karen E. Smith, *European Union Foreign Policy. A Changing World* (Malden: Polity Press, 2008), p. 211.

8 Rajendra Kumar Jain, "Fortifying the 'Fortress': Immigration and Politics in the European Union," *International Studies* (New Delhi), 1996, pp. 163-192; Kamal Mitra Chenoy, and Anuradha M. Chenoy, "India´s Foreign Policy Shifts and the Calculus of Power," *Economic and Political Weekly*, 42(35), September 2007, p. 3551.

9 Klaus-Gerd Giesen, *L'éthiques des relations internationales. Les théories anglo-américaines contemporaines* (Brussels: Bruylant, 1992), pp. 46, 78, 322.

10 Hartmut Elsenhans, "Political Obstacles to Private Sector Development," in James G. Bennett, ed., *Private Sector Development in Bangladesh* (Cologne: Oase, 1991), p. 211.

11 André Drainville, "Québec City 2001 and the Making of Transnational Subjects," *Socialist Register*, 38, 2002 pp. 21ff; Ronnie D. Lipschutz, "Power, Politics and Global Civil Society," *Millennium: Journal of International Studies*, 33(3), June 2005, p. 753; Issa G. Shivji, "The Silences in the NGO Discourse: The Role and Future of NGOs in Africa,"

Africa Development, 31(4), 2006, p. 44.

12 Hartmut Elsenhans, *State, Class and Development* (New Delhi: Radiant; London: Sangam Books, 1996), esp. pp. 178ff.

13 Ignacio Sánchez-Cuenca, "The Political Basis of Support for European Integration," *European Union Politics*, 1(2), 2000, p. 147; Michael Bruter, "Developments in the Member States," *Journal of Common Market Studies*, 42, Supplement 1, September 2004, p. 144.

14 T.K. Oommen, "Insiders and Outsiders in India: Primordial Collectivism and Cultural Pluralism in Nation-Building," *International Sociology*, 1(1), March 1986, p. 63.

15 Michael Gehler and Wolfram Kaiser, "Transnationalism and Early European Integration: The Nouvelles Equipes Internationales and the Geneva Circle 1947-1957," *Historical Journal*, 44(3), 2001, pp. 776ff.

16 Anke Jacobsen and Horst Tomann, "Europäische Währungsunion und Lohnpolitik," *Hamburger Jahrbücher für Wirtschafts- und Gesellschaftspolitik*, 43 (1998), p. 212; Kolja Möller, "Gouvernementales Wahrheitsregime oder dezentrales Netzwerk-Regieren?Die europäische Beschäftigungsstrategie als Machtökonomie," *Leviathan*, 37(4), December 2009, pp. 575-601; Arne Heise, "Boosting Employment through Coordinated Macro Policies: A Viable Option for the EU?," Michael Dauderstädt, and Lothar Witte, eds., *Work and Welfare in the Enlarging Euroland* (Bonn: Friedrich Ebert Stiftung, 2002), pp. 63ff.

17 Kenneth A. Armstrong, "Rediscovering Civil Society: The European Union and the White Paper on Governance," *European Law Journal*, 8(1), March 2002, p. 106.

18 Jutta Joachim and Matthias Dembinski, "A Contradiction in Terms? NGOs, Democracy, and European Foreign and Security Policy," *Journal of European Public Policy*, 18(8), 2011, p. 1162; Robert Dover, "From CFSP to ESDP: The EU's Foreign, Security, and Defence Policies," Michelle Cini, and Nieves Pérez-Solórzano Borragán, eds., *European Union Politics* (Cambridge, Mass.: Oxford University Press, 2010), p. 256; Jens von Schaik and Simon Schunz, "Explaining EU Activism and Impact in Global Climate Politics: Is the Union a Norm- or Interest-Driven Actor?," *Journal of Common Market Studies*, 50(1), 2012, p. 177.

19 Thomas Risse, "The Euro Between National and European Identity," *Journal of European Public Policy*, 10(4), August 2003, pp. 487-495; Hartmut Elsenhans, "European Union's External Relations: Nature, Priorities, and Issues," in Jayaraj Amin, ed., *European Union in a Changing International Order* (Delhi: Kaveri 2013).

20 Karris Muller, "'Concentric Circles' at the Periphery of the European Union," *Australian Journal of Politics and History*, 46(3), September 2000,

p. 323; P.H. Liotta and Taylor Owen, *Europe Takes on Human Security. INEF Report 80* (Duisburg: Institut für Entwicklung und Frieden, 2006), p. 75; Claudia Major, *EU-UN Cooperation in Military Crisis Management: The Experience of EUFOR RD Congo in 2006. Occasional Paper 72* (Paris: European Union Institute for Security Studies), September 2008, p. 9; Wanda Troszcynska-van Genderen, "Human Rights Challenges in EU Civilian Crisis Management: The Cases of EUPOL and EUJUST LEX," *Occasional Paper 84* (Paris: Institute for Security Studies, August 2010), pp.13f.

21 Rajendra Kumar Jain, "The European Union and China: Indian Perceptions and Perspectives," *European Studies: A Journal of European Culture, History and Politics*, 27(2), 2009, p. 146; Álvaro de Vasconcelos, *A Strategy for EU Foreign Policy. Report 7* (Paris: Institute for Security Studies, June 2010), p. 71; Pramit Pal Chaudhuri, "India, Europe and the Rise of Asia," in this volume.

22 Gisela Hendriks and Annette Morgan, *The Franco-German Axis in European Integration* (Cheltenham: Edward Elgar, 2001), p. 161; Stanley Hoffman, "Towards a Common European Foreign and Security Policy?," *Journal of Common Market Studies*, 38(2), 2000, p. 1983.

23 "How Orthodox is the Mainstream? Economic Theory and Economic Policy Advice in the English-Speaking Area," *Intervention*, 4(1), 2007, pp. 8-12.

24 Jan Turowski, *Sozialdemokratische Reformdiskurse* (Wiesbaden: VS Verlag für Sozialwissenschaften, 2010), p. 61.

25 Klaus Busch, *Gewerkschaftliche Tarifpolitik in Europa – Handlungsbedingungen und -möglichkeiten in alternativen Integrationsszenarien. Expertise im Auftrage der Han-Böckler-Stiftung* (Osnabrück, 1993), p. 12; Philip Arestis and Malcolm Sawyer, "Prospects for the Single European Currency and Some Proposals for a New Maastricht," in Paul Davidson and Jan Kregel, eds., *Full Employment and Price Stability in a Global Economy* (Cheltenham: Edward Elgar, 1999), p. 73.

26 Hartmut Elsenhans, *The Rise and Demise of the Capitalist World System* (Leipzig: Leipziger Universitätsverlag, 2011), p. 120.

27 Hartmut Elsenhans, "Finanzkrise als Chance? Die Entstehung fiktiven Reichtums," *Welt Trends*, 18(71), March/April 2010, p. 100; Hartmut Elsenhans, "Finanzkrise und Staatsintervention. Warum wurden Chancen der Regulierung verpasst," in Ayad Al-Ani, ed., *Widerstand in Organisationen. Organisationen im Widerstand* (Berlin: Springer, 2013), forthcoming.

28 Peter Bofinger, Jürgen Habermas, and Julian Nida-Rümelin, "Plus que jamais, l'Europe," *Le Monde*, 27 August 2012, p. 12.

4

India, the European Union and Global Norms

V.G. Hegde

Introduction

India and the European Union have been pursuing and supporting the establishment and formulation of a certain set of global norms and standards based on their perception and understanding of the larger world.[1] This pursuit is based on their aspiration to be part of the larger and wider world without essentially disregarding their regional identities. In fact, these regional identities of both the EU and India mould their respective approaches towards developing the contours of these global norms and standards. European identity primarily shapes the Union's approach towards all global issues, including the creation of global norms and standards. India, on the other hand, defines and seeks to identify its regional identity in the larger context of the developing world, although its immediate concerns relate to South Asia. Thus, both India and EU seek to identify, understand and enforce global norms and standards from their own perspective which is essentially linked to their regional identities.

While India and the EU have their own preferences and hierarchy for prioritizing these global norms, the presumption is that global norms and standards do not exist in a vacuum. In fact, they exist or get extinct on account of several factors. The foremost factor for the sustenance of a global norm is its wider usage and practice by at least a sizeable number of States within the international community. A global norm might become extinct if a certain number of powerful States decide not to adhere to it or to put it to consistent disuse. There is an argument that global norms and standards do not need the same kind of adherence as required for core international legal principles.[2] Substantive compliance by a certain number of States should suffice to meet the prevalence of a global norm or standard. Considering their importance and influence within the international community, the approach and perception of both India and the EU towards a specific emerging global norm and standard would be crucial. This chapter examines some of these aspects in relation to India and the European Union.

Historical Context

The EU is a continent by itself and its growing and influential role in world politics needs no further elaboration.[3] Besides hosting three permanent members of the United Nations Security Council, the Union has been an active participant in all global negotiations.[4] It has also argued that "modern international law is to a large extent a European invention".[5] European States are also said to have had "a dominant influence on the development of international law for many centuries in contemporary history".[6] In terms of its size and population, India can also be regarded as a continent by itself with its civilizational attribution, a large population, diverse languages and culture.[7] In economic terms, it is now an emerging economy and has carved out for itself a crucial role in all major global negotiations.[8] Considering this profile, both India and the EU seek to approach issues at the global level, be it legal or non-legal, with a certain degree of responsibility taking into account their own historical and regional realities. However, they seem to have divergent views and emphases on the kinds of global norms they wish to support and actualize. This dichotomous approach, is reflected in the process of norm creation as well. Several historical reasons explain the evolution of such different approaches.

India's colonial past and the ideals of the freedom movement have apparently essentially shaped and influenced its foreign policy goals.[9] Others argue that this is no longer the case since India has now adopted a more pragmatic approach.[10] Independent India joined the group of developing countries and sought to espouse their concerns and causes in diverse fora. Since the end of the Second World War, India and its emerging international legal scholarship legitimately argued for the major concerns of the developing world and in the process questioned the Eurocentric notion of creation of global norms.[11] A seminar discourse in this regard argues that the majority of the developing countries, including India, remained, at the periphery of the process of the creation of global norms.[12] Many leading scholars of developing countries have, therefore, sought to challenge the process of global norm creation in which a majority of developing countries have no role to play.[13] Therefore, India does not accept certain global norms, which evolved and existed since the end of the Second World War, since it had no role in their creation. In recent years, India seems to adhere to this approach. However, it has been increasingly adopting a more pragmatic approach towards global legal and policy issues in order to vigorously pursue its own national interests.

The European Union, on the other hand, pursues its agenda on global norms by taking into account its own basic parameters which have evolved and are premised on the belief that Europe has been primarily responsible for the creation of these global norms. For centuries, the Eurocentric nature of global norms, as we understand them today, was accepted as an accomplished fact. It is only in recent decades, however, that the Eurocentric nature of global norms has been increasingly challenged.

Both India and the EU today pursue their global agenda in specific contexts.[14] For India, Asia (South Asia specifically) provides the historical and political context. Decolonization, the declaration and the establishment of a New International Economic Order (NIEO), negotiations relating to the development of international legal regimes for the sea and a number of other international legal issues, mainly concerning developing countries, have occupied Indian attention for nearly three decades. However, respect for international law is one of the basic tenets of India's approach. Article 51(c) of the Indian Constitution specifically provides for "fostering respect" for international law and treaty obligations undertaken by India. The Indian Constitution also provides for the settlement of all disputes through negotiations and peaceful means, preferably by arbitration.[15]

For the EU, Europe as a whole provides the specific context for its approach towards norm creation. As a geographical entity, Europe has been gradually expanding. The Lisbon Treaty clearly seeks to outline the global norms in relation to a wider world while protecting its own values and interests. Article 3(5) of the Lisbon Treaty, *inter alia* lists these global norms as "peace, security, the sustainable development of the Earth, solidarity and mutual respect among peoples, free and fair trade, eradication of poverty and the protection of human rights, in particular rights of the child, as well as to the strict observance and the development of international law, including the respect for the principles of the United Nations Charter".[16]

Global Norms as Soft Law Instruments

The process of norm creation in world politics is a complex process. International legal norms usually take a long time to evolve. Before such norms become binding hard law norms, they often begin their life as soft law instruments.[17] At any given point of time, very few norms attain the status of hard and binding legal norms at the global level. States are bound to follow such binding norms. There can be no derogation from that. Many of the norms at the international level could be regarded as 'soft law' norms embodied in soft law instruments.[18] States find it easier to accept these soft law instruments. They provide States flexible space to implement and enforce such evolving norms and standards. Such soft law norms could be varied and would be at different stages of evolution. Both India and the EU have been pursuing and are supporting these soft law norms, which can be broadly termed as "global norms and standards", as part of their national policy frameworks.[19]

Global hard law regimes need no support either from India or the EU. Hard law norms relating to the international criminal justice system, e.g. crimes against humanity, crime of genocide and war crimes require no support either from India or the EU as these norms bind all States at the global level.[20] Hard law norms could be regarded as *jus cogens*, i.e. peremptory norm under international law. The list of hard law norms would continue to grow. Both India and the EU generally adhere to and enforce these norms. However, they have their own priorities in the pursuit or support of some of these norms and standards taking into account their own national and regional realities. Similarly, soft law norms are equally crucial as they act as signpost towards the evolution of future binding norms.

This chapter seeks to examine and limit itself, albeit briefly, to the study of the approach and perceptions of the EU and India about certain global norms and standards as created or pursued within the framework of the United Nations.[21] This, no doubt, is a broad yet a limited framework, although global norms and standards pervade various aspects of global and inter-state relations. Above all, these norms and standards attain a critical role at different levels and are pursued by States at local, sub-regional, regional and global levels. Given their importance, both India and the EU, as stated earlier, will have to situate themselves at all these levels and will pursue their respective preferences in the support of certain specific norms and standards which are inevitable within the UN context. The next section seeks to examine the preferences of India and the EU and the divergence and convergence in their approaches towards global norms.

Norms and Standards in the UN Context

One of the basic elements in global norm creation relates to its institutional aspect. At the global level, the United Nations provides this institutional, legal and political framework, although there are many other kinds of specialized bodies (within and outside the UN system) that provide a basic framework to a certain extent. However, all the different multilateral treaty bodies at the global level concern the UN in the broader context of "maintenance of international peace and security".[22] Thus, the United Nations plays a pre-eminent role in the international community of States towards norm creation and its sustenance. Both India and the EU approach and seek to shape various aspects of the UN norm creation process in accordance with their national and regional perspectives and priorities. The role of the United Nations in global norm creation needs no specific analysis[23] as it facilitates norm creation in terms of both soft law and hard law. A bird's view of the United Nations shows us that there is a continuous process at play with regard to norm creation specifically within the UN General Assembly.[24] Several such norms are at different stages of evolution within the UN. States accord a higher or lower status to many of these global norms as they deem fit. Both India and the EU approach these norms taking into account their own national and regional priorities.

Institutional Aspects

Both India and EU tend to approach the institutional aspects of the UN and its reform process with caution.[25] India argues for an institutional framework within the UN which "should reflect contemporary realities". Its emphasis is on strengthening the UN General Assembly as it provides a forum of wider discussion. India seeks "better reporting mechanism" and "change in the composition" of the UN Security Council. India has also been advocating an increase in the both permanent and non-permanent members UN Security Council and wants "no distinction between in voting between permanent and non-permanent members". EU, on its part, seeks to emphasise the "role of UN in global governance" and supports a "stronger multilateral system" that could facilitate "preventive diplomacy". The Union's references to UN reforms have been summed up with its call for the "revitalization" of the UN General Assembly and the UN Security Council. "Strengthening the UN based on effective and sustainable funding – in line with real capacity to pay, and increasing the efficiency of its functioning –," Brussels argues, "remain our top priorities." For the EU, revitalization means "a more streamlined, more accountable and more effective General Assembly at dealing with the issues currently on its agenda."[26]

Rule of Law and the Protection of Civilians

The EU has been advocating ideas relating to 'rule of law' within the UN. It urges greater "accountability" and demands to "bring perpetrators of international crime to book". The Union also argues for strengthening of the International Criminal Court (ICC) and urges those those nations which have not yet joined ICC to do so.[27] India has not so far joined ICC it since it has many apprehensions about some of these concepts. It has introduced and supported a resolution on the "Rule of Law" and since 2005 the issue of "Responsibility to Protect" (R2P). EU has a "narrow but deep approach to R2P" and "welcomes references to R2P in UNSC resolutions of 1970, 1973 and 1975 of 2011".

The EU has recently been placing greater emphasis on the

"protection of civilians" and has linked this concept to R2P. Ninety per cent of casualties in contemporary armed conflicts, Brussels argues, are civilians and 10 per cent combatants. "Protection of civilians" is, therefore, crucial. The EU argues that R2P has, in fact, been an "intransgressible principle of customary international law". To that end, it refers to some of the averments made by the International Court of Justice in this regard. The EU goes one step further in advocating the "duty to protect civilians not only during international armed conflicts, but also during national strifes".

India does not accept this broad interpretation and has been cautious in accepting these concepts as "intransgressible principles". India and Indian international legal scholars have been critical of the EU's position. They have stressed that both R2P and the ideas and norms relating to "protection of civilians" have been put forward to justify what had earlier been termed as "humanitarian intervention", which has always been controversial. Justifications for such acts of interventions under international law have been widely criticized both in terms of law and fact. By such ideas and norms, the EU seeks to broaden the concept of "peacekeeping".[28] India is not in favour of such broad interpretations given to some of these concepts, which have been included in resolutions of the UN General Assembly and UN Security Council with prospects of broad interpretations. Some of these recent resolutions, [29] especially those of the UN Security Council have been criticized.

Peacekeeping

There seems to be some convergence between India and the EU regarding peacekeeping. Both agree that peacekeeping operations should be strengthened and that more female peacekeepers should be inducted. The Union, however, has a more specific agenda in this regard when it refers to "peace-building". Brussels has been advocating the establishment of a Special Committee on Peacekeeping Operations within the

Security Council in order to make it more a practical and on-going issue. The EU also argues that as regards peacekeeping "we are beyond the conceptual stage". It goes much beyond traditional ideas of peacekeeping and has proposed the establishment of a "Peace-building Commission". India concurs that "peacekeeping-peacebuilding are and will remain core activities of the United Nations in times to come".[30] It feels that while "peacebuilding is a cooperative and collective effort", there is an imperative need to augment financial resources through international financial institutions. It also stresses development of "the normative basis for peacebuilding" with specific focus on security sector reform, rule of law, developmental quests, economic recovery and employment generation.

International Environmental Law

India and the European Union have some convergence on environmental issues. New Delhi often refers to its own proactive role in taking initiatives within the global community to evolve a consensus on major global environmental issues.[31] However, it primarily takes up these issues in the context of fostering the development and aspirations of developing countries. India has been a party to several of the multilateral environmental agreements.[32] It is among the top 12 mega centres of the world in terms of genetic diversity. India has expressed disappointment over the lack of fulfillment of international commitments undertaken voluntarily by the industrialized countries at Rio which includes EU as well. However, both India and the EU agree that closer international cooperation is essential in the field of environment in order to effectively deal with global environmental problems. Both are committed to global partnership.

Counter-Terrorism

International terrorism has been and continues to be a major concern for India.[33] Besides supporting other international legal initiatives in this area, India submitted its draft of the Comprehensive Convention on International Terrorism (CCIT) to the Ad Hoc Committee of the UN General Assembly on International Terrorism in 1996 and has been consistently arguing for its passage to comprehensively address the issue of terrorism. Among the important issues relating to the CCIT that India focuses on include (a) the need to take into account the lawful exercise of the right of peoples to self-determination; (b) the need to capture concerns relating to 'state terrorism'; (c) resolution of matters concerning potential impunity of military forces; and (d) the need to delineate activities to be covered by the scope of the Convention and those covered by humanitarian instruments.[34] The CCIT has, however, been held somewhat hostage to definitions of certain conceptual ideas, which India does not welcome. The EU has been supporting negotiations on the CCIT and it remains a priority for both sides. However, while supporting such counter-terrorism strategies, Brussels has been emphasizing "respect of international law, human rights and the rule of law".[35]

Both EU and India have welcomed the adoption of the "UN Global Counter Terrorism Strategy of 2006" that recognized the need to express solidarity with innocent victims and specifically addressed victims of terrorism. India also referred to certain practical measures such as extradition, prosecution, information exchange and capacity building. The EU has separate standards for the implementation of some of these practical measures relating to extradition[36], death sentence and other related issues. The two sides have also been been working together through a Joint Working Group on Terrorism.

Human Rights

Human rights form an integral part of EU's broader strategy and work programme and pervade all its major activities. According to the EU, they are "inextricably linked" to other goals of the United Nations on security and development. Brussels reiterates that it will "continue to counter efforts by third parties to undermine the respect for universality of human rights notably with regard to human rights and cultural diversity and defamation of religions".[37] The Union has been supporting several initiatives relating to the rights of the child, independence of the Human Rights Council, and of Special Procedures, including country-specific and thematic mandates. It also devotes special attention to respect for the universality of human rights, mainstreaming of gender perspectives, empowerment of women, and the promotion of participation of civil society.

India, on the other hand, advocates a "holistic and integrated approach that gives equal emphasis to all human rights, based on their interdependence, inter-relatedness, indivisibility and universality and reinforces the inter-relationship between democracy, development, human rights and international cooperation for development".[38] Both India and EU are committed to make the Human Rights Council a strong, effective and efficient body capable of promoting and protecting human rights and fundamental freedoms for all.[39]

Conclusion

India and the European Union have been actively engaged in global norm creation through various processes, specifically through soft law instruments. This chapter has sought to define and understand global norms and standards in a broader perspective to include various issues such as (a) international trade law issues and other related standards; (b) international environmental issues and the norms created pursuant to that; (c) human rights issues and various global norms created to realize and actualize these norms; and (d) issues relating to the implementation and working of the international humanitarian law and related issues.

This chapter has discussed the historical contexts in which both India and the EU are situated as well as the norm creation process within the UN system, peacekeeping, international environmental law, counter-terrorism and human rights. Both India and the EU have been working together at the bilateral level in an effort to find areas of convergence and find common threads to work together on many common global issues.[40] Apart from close bilateral ties, the two sides are members of several groupings such as G20 and the Asia Europe Meeting (ASEM). In some instances, India has been an Observer or a Special Invitee some special meetings. The growing importance of India on account of its political stability (as a democracy) and economic growth as well as its traditional proactive role in multilateral negotiations makes it an important country in global norm creation process. Both the EU and India have been in close touch with each other concerning various economic issues at both the G8 and G20.

Even within the World Trade Organization, India and the EU have sought to closely coordinate their positions even though there have wide divergences on various trade and other related issues. On norms relating to economic issues, the Union has been pushing for a broad policy framework in several areas, viz. (a) addressing economic imbalances; (b) reform of financial markets; (c) a single set of global accounting standards (the Basel Banking Regulations – Basel I and Basel II – are in place and have been adopted by India); (d) increasing the role of the International Monetary Fund to contain economic difficulties (while the Union supports it; India has different views and does not agree entirely); and (e) the introduction of a Global Financial Transaction Tax. India and the European Union need to more closely examine these issues, especially in the context of the ongoing economic and Eurozone sovereign debt crisis.

NOTES

1 In this chapter, reference to 'global norms' includes both the 'global norms and standards'. Norms, especially customary norms, are binding on all States under international law. Standards, on the other hand, are created with view to bring in an uniformity of approach and application. It should be noted that 'norms and standards' could be developed outside the State structures and accordingly this terminology under international law has been accorded a broad meaning. For example, there are agreed trade norms and standards under various World Trade Organization (WTO) Agreements. At the same time, many of the WTO agreements refer to specific standards that are applicable or to be implemented by the Members States (www.wto.org). The World Health Organization (WHO) seeks to provide safety and quality assurance of medicines through development and promotion of international norms and standards, guidelines and nomenclature. See www.who.int/medicines/areas/quality-sa. About the process of norm creation within the United Nations, generally see, Jose E. Alvarez, *International Organizations as Law-Makers* (Oxford: Oxford University Press, 2005). "These norms," according to one view, "strictly circumscribe the conditions under which States can participate in and authorize these activities and proscribe all involvement by non-state actors. Those who refuse or fail to conform are labeled as deviants and condemned not just by States but by most communities and individuals as well." See Ethan A. Nadelmann, "Global Prohibition Regimes: The Evolution of Norms in International Society," *International Organization*, 44(4), Autumn 1990, pp. 479-526.

2 International legal principles evolve over a long period of time through widespread State practice and accordingly the majority of States feel that they are bound by it. Such international legal principles are termed as "customary norms of international law". For a detailed account of some of these basic international norm creation processes, see Malcolm N. Shah, *International Law* (Cambridge: Cambridge University Press, 1997) p. 68.

3 See generally http://europa.eu/about-eu/basic-information.

4 The EU has been part of all international trade and other negotiations. As an original member of the General Agreement on Trade and Tariffs (GATT) and later the World Trade Organization negotiations and in its Ministerial Meetings, it has played a crucial role. In fact, GATT was its idea in the post-Second World War reconstruction along with other

global financial institutions. It also played a major role in climate change negotiations. In a way, it is impossible to think about the current global order without acknowledge the important role of the EU.

5 Jan Wouters, Andre Nollkaemper and Erika de Wet, eds., *The Europeanisation of International Law: The Status of International Law in the EU and Its Member States* (The Hague: T.M.C. Asser Press, 2008), p. 4.

6 However, there are conflicting views about such a dominance and scholars even within Europe argue for a more inclusive approach. See generally, A. Orakhelashvili, "The Idea of European International Law," *European Journal of International Law*, 17, 2006, p. 315; M. Koskenniemi, "International Law in Europe: between Tradition and Renewal," *European Journal of International Law*, 16, 2005, pp. 113-124.

7 See generally http://india.gov.in/knowindia/profile.php. Also see R. P. Anand, *Development of Modern International Law and India* (Berlin: Nomos Publishers, 2005); B.S. Chimni, "Alternative Visions of Just World Order: Six Tales from India," *Harvard International Law Journal,* Summer 2005, 46(2), pp. 389-402.

8 The Indian subcontinent is much larger than the EU both in terms of population and size. India has also been the cradle of an ancient civilization in Asia. A diverse culture, languages and major religions emerged from India. India has been aspiring to become a permanent member of the UN Security Council. In the past six decades, it was elected six times as a non-permanent member of the Security Council to serve two years each time. For an account of India's quest to be part of the UN Security Council and the assessment of its performance as a non-permanent member, see C.S.R. Murthy, "India's Non-Permanent Membership in the UN Security Council," in Ankush B. Sawant, ed., *Sixty Years of India's Contribution to the United Nations* (New Delhi: Authorspress, 2010), p. 39.

9 M.S. Rajan, *India and Making of the UN Charter in United Nations and World Politics* (1995), p. 315; R.P. Anand, "Jawaharlal Nehru and International Law and Relations," in R.P Anand, ed., *Studies in International Law and History: An Asian Perspective* (New Delhi: Lancer's Books, 2004), p. 16; M. Sahovic, "Nehru's Ideas and the Future of International Law," *Indian Journal of International Law*, 29, 1989, p. 94.

10 According to 'realists', "in a strife and conflict-ridden world what is paramount importance is the safeguarding of national security interests. The UN system can at best be one of the several elements in meeting this objective. This explains why India is constructing a network of strategic partnerships with the United States, Russia, the European

Union, China and Japan". See Purushottam Bhattacharya, "Adapting to a Changing World: Indian Approach to the United Nations in the Early 21st Century," in Sawant, n. 8, p. 366; also see, Nalini Kant Jha, ed., *India's Foreign Policy in a Changing World* (New Delhi: South Asian Publishers, 2000).

11 C.H. Alexandrowicz, "Kautilyan Principles and the Law of Nations," *British Year Book of International Law*, 41, 1965–66, p. 301; C.H. Alexandrowicz, *An Introduction to the History of the Law of Nations in the East Indies (16th, 17th and 18th Centuries)* (Oxford: Clarendon Press, 1967); R.P. Anand, New *States and International Law* (New Delhi: Vikas, 1972); M. Sornarajah, "The Asian Perspective to International Law in the Age of Globalization," *Singapore Journal of International and Comparative Law*, 5, 2001, p. 284; P.C. Jessup, "Diversity and Uniformity in the Law of Nations," *American Journal of International Law*, 58, 1964, p. 351. The *Indian Journal of International Law* has published several articles on this issue since its inception in 1960. Some of them could be noted here: C.J. Chacko, "International Law in India: Ancient India," *Indian Journal of International Law*, 1, 1960, p. 184 (published in two parts); N. Singh, "International Law in India: Mediaeval India," *Indian Journal of International Law*, 2, 1962, p. 65 (published in three parts).

12 The European origin of several international legal norms relating to Law of the Sea has been questioned. See R.P. Anand, *Origin and Development of the Law of the Sea: History of International Law Revisited* (The Hague: Martinus Nijhoff, 1983). On the creation of norms relating to intellectual property and related areas and the role of India and other developing countries, see V.G. Hegde, "India and International Patent System," in Bimal Patel, ed., *India and International Law* (Leiden: Koninklijke Brill, 2005); R.P. Anand, *Development of Modern International Law and India* (Berlin: Nomos Publishers, 2005); B.S. Chimni," Asian Civilizations and International Law: Some Reflections," *Asian Journal of International Law*, 1(1), January 2011, pp. 19-42; also see M. Koskenniemi, *The Gentle Civilizer of Nations: The Rise and Fall of International Law 1870-1960* (Cambridge: 2001); Onuma Yasuaki "When was the Law of International Society Born? An Inquiry of the History of International Law from an Intercivilisational Perspective," *Journal of the History of International Law*, 2, 2000.

13 R.P. Anand, "Attitude of the Asian-African States toward Certain Problems of International Law," *International and Comparative Law Quarterly*, 15(1), 1966, p. 56; M. Mushkat, "The African Approach to Some Basic Problems of Modern International Law," *Indian Journal of*

International Law, 7, 1967), p. 335; R. Khan, "International Law: Old and New," *Indian Journal of International Law*, 15, 1975, p. 371.

14 Some of these bilateral initiatives could be noted. According to a report by India, the 1994 Cooperation Agreement signed between EU and India took bilateral relations well beyond trade and economic cooperation. Further, the fifth India-EU Summit at The Hague in 2004 endorsed the EU's proposal to upgrade its relationship with India to a "strategic partnership". The two sides also adopted a Joint Action Plan in 2005 which provides for strengthening dialogues and consultative mechanisms; deepening political dialogue and cooperation. The report also refers to several bilateral agreements signed between India and the EU. These are: Cooperation in the Field of Science and Technology in 2001 and the same was renewed in 2007; Joint Vision Statement for Promoting Cooperation in the Field of Information and Communication Technology in 2001; Customs Cooperation Agreement in 2004; Memorandum of Understanding on Cooperation on Employment and Social Affairs in November 2006; Horizontal Civil Aviation Agreement in 2008; Joint Declaration in the Field of Education in 2008; Joint Declaration on Multilinguism in March 2009; and Agreement in the Field of Nuclear Fusion Energy and Research in November 2009; and Joint Declaration on Culture in 2010. See *India-EU Relations* (Ministry of External Affairs: Government of India) http://www.mea.gov.in/staticfile/EUJan2012.

15 Text of Article 51(c) of the Constitution provides: "The State shall endeavour to (a) promote international peace and security; (b) maintain just and honourable relations between nations; (c) foster respect for international law and treaty obligations in the dealings of the organized peoples with one another; and(d) encourage settlement of international disputes by arbitration."

16 The treaty of Lisbon amending the Treaty of European Union and the Treaty establishing the European Community, was signed at Lisbon on 13 December 2007. This Treaty entered into force on 1 December 2009. The Treaty of Lisbon amends the current EU and EC treaties, without replacing them. It provides the Union with the legal framework and tools necessary to meet future challenges and to respond to citizens' demands. One of the main goals is to promote human rights both internally and around the world. Human dignity, freedom, democracy, equality, the rule of law and respect for human rights: these are the core values of the EU. See generally http://europa.eu/about-eu/basic.information; also see summary of the speech made by Maros

Sefcovic, Vice President of the European Commission Responsible for Interinstitutional Relations and Administration on "The Treaty of Lisbon – One year on Cooperation in a Mature Institutional Framework," at the European University Institute, 12 November 2010 (available at http://europa.eu.)

17 Generally under international law there is a distinction between 'hard law' and 'soft law' norm. Hard law norms, such as treaties, customs and agreements provide binding obligations for States. While soft law norms provide flexible non-binding obligations thereby allowing States time to adjust their domestic legal and other concerns. Resolutions of the United Nations General Assembly and of other international organizations, principles, declarations and regulations could be regarded as part of soft law. On an account of this distinction between hard and soft law and the role played by them in norm creation under international law, see generally P.S. Rao, "The Role of Soft Law in the Development of International Law: Some Random Notes," in *Commemorative Essays on International Law* (New Delhi: Asian-African Legal Consultative Organization, 2007).

18 Many environment-related principles such as 'precautionary principle, inter-generation equity' and other similar principles could be regarded as 'soft law' instruments. In a future date, these principles may attain the status of hard law with widespread and uniform State practice.

19 The available literature and reference to soft law instruments and their interpretation is varied and many. They even include norms created by local courts and other civil society organizations. See Balakrishnan Rajagopal, *International Law From Below: Development, Social Movements and Third World Resistance* (Cambridge: Cambridge University Press, 2003); B.S. Chimni, "Globalization, Humanitarianism and the Erosion of Refugee Protection," *Journal of Refugee Studies,* 13(3), September 2000, pp. 243-263; David Weissbrodt and Muria Kruger, "Norms on the Responsibilities of Transnational Corporations and Other Business Enterprises with regard to Human Rights," *The American Journal of International Law*, 97(4), October 2003, p. 901; Yishai Blank, "Localism in the New Global Legal Order," *Harvard International Law Journal*, 47, 2006, p. 263; Ramesh Thakur "Global Norms and International Humanitarian Law: An Asian Perspective," *International Review of the Red Cross*, No.841, 2001, pp. 19-41; Graeme B. Dinwoodie, "A New Copyright Order: Why National Courts should Create Global Norms," *University of Pennsylvania Review*, 149, 2000, p. 469.

20 Some of the hard law norms get incorporated into treaties. See for

example, various provisions in the Statute of International Criminal Court, specifically relating to the definition of crimes.

21 The UN has a larger mandate under the rubric of 'peace and security'. The EU document outlining its priorities for the 67th Session of the UN General Assembly, for example, lists the following: peacekeeping; role of regional organizations in the multilevel governance; respect for humanitarian principles, human rights law and refugee law; concept of protection of civilians; peacebuildling; responsibility to protect; preventive diplomacy and mediation; human security; participation of women in peace processes; protection of children in armed conflict; promotion of rule of law both at the national and international level; multilateral disarmament negotiations; universalizing safeguards regimes relating atomic energy and to ensure application of International Atomic Energy Agency's (IAEA) safety standards and security guidelines; adoption of International Code of Conduct on Outer Space Activities; Transnational Organized Crimes; Corruption; Drug Control Measures; Piracy; Sustainable Development (Rio+20); Climate Change; and Human Rights. See http://www.eu-un.europa.eu. India also approaches majority of these issues and the norms standards created in relation to these subjects with its own perception. India, for instance, seeks to support norms relating to revitalization issues of the UN; issues relating to global counter-terrorism; sustainable development; human security; post-conflict peacebuilding; gender equality and empowerment of women.

22 Article 103 of the UN Charter specifies that "In the event of a conflict between the obligations of the Member of the United Nations under the present Charter and their obligations under any other agreement, their obligations under the present Charter shall prevail."

23 See Benedetto Conforti, *The Law and Practice of the United Nations* (Leiden: Martinus Nijhoff: 2005); also see V.S. Mani, "The Role of Law and Legal Considerations in the Functioning of the United Nations," in M.S. Rajan, ed., *United Nations at Fifty and Beyond* (New Delhi: Indian Society of International Law, 1996); M.S. Rajan, *Expanding Jurisdiction of the United Nations* (Bombay: N.M. Tripathi, 1982); Rosalyn Higgins, *The Development of International Law through the Political Organs of the United Nations* (London: Oxford University Press, 1963); Alvarez E. Jose, *International Organizations as Law-Makers* (Oxford: Oxford University Press, 2005).

24 The resolutions passed by the UN General Assembly every year run into several hundred pages and the range of issues covered by them is

immense. It has been argued by several international law scholars that some of these resolutions passed over several years could constitute or give recourse to the formation of a binding norm, keeping in view the constant State practice.

25 On the issue of UN reform process, both India and the EU have been making statements both within UNGA and UNSC. For the EU statements and priorities, see http://www.eu-un.europa.eu. For the Indian statements see http://www.un.int/india. These statements are made in the United Nations' Ad Hoc Working Group on the Revitalization of the General Assembly.

26 http://www.eu-un.europa.eu.

27 Ibid.

28 EU supports the UNSC Resolution 1894 on this issue. The resolution on "Protection of Civilians in Armed Conflicts" was adopted by the UN Security Council on 11 November 2009, S/RES/1894 (2009).

29 Specifically on Afghanistan, Libya, Syria (though not passed by UNSC), the idea of 'no-fly zone' and the possibilities for the wider interpretation of the resolution (and consequent action) have led to wider criticism.

30 Statement by India on Post-Conflict Peacebuilding at the UN General Assembly Plenary on 19 March 2012 responding to the Report of the Peacebuilding Commission on its fifth session. See http://www.un.int/india.

31 It has been noted in the Indian statement that the then Prime Minister of India, Mrs. Indira Gandhi, was the sole foreign head of State or government to participate in the UN Conference on Human Environment held in Stockholm in June 1972.

32 These include the Framework Convention on Climate Change, the Convention on Biological Diversity, the Vienna Convention on the Protection of the Ozone Layer, the Montreal Protocol on Substances that Deplete the Ozone Layer, the Ramsar Convention on Wetlands of International Importance, the Basel Convention on the Transboundary Movement of Hazardous Wastes, the Convention on Combating Desertification and the Convention on the International Trade in Endangered Species of Wild Flora and Fauna.

33 India is a party to all the 13 major UN instruments relating to specific terrorist activities.

34 For the Indian views on the subject, see generally www.un.int/india_counter_terrorism.html.

35 The EU has been arguing for the promotion of 'human security' as a comprehensive, integrated and people-centred approach in addressing

interrelated threats to security, livelihood and dignity of people and vulnerable communities. See generally www.europa-eu-un.org/articles/articleslist_s110_en.htm.

36 It is generally accepted that the norm 'extradite or prosecute' has not yet been crystallized into customary norm of international law. Extradition arrangements are usually done through bilateral agreements and arrangements. There is no multilateral framework as yet for the extradition issues, except for some soft law instruments.

37 See www. europa-eu-un.org/articles/articleslist_s110-en.htm.

38 See www.un.int/india/india-and-the-un-hr.html.

39 Ibid. India makes a specific reference to UN Convention on the Rights of Persons with Disabilities. India signed and ratified this Convention immediately after its adoption. Both India and EU also have similar positions on the adoption and implementation of Convention on the Rights of the Child.

40 Both India and the EU have been negotiating a Free Trade Agreement and its negotiation continues to remain inconclusive. Further work is required in particular on tariffs, services and procurement (including work on non-tariff barriers). Recently EU Trade Commissioner Karel De Gucht and Indian Commerce Minister Anand Sharma expressed their satisfaction that negotiations towards an EU-India ambitious Free Trade Agreement are making good progress. See *Joint Statement on the Outcome of the EU-India Trade Ministerial,* 26 June 2012 at http://trade.ec.europa.eu.

5

India, the European Union and Peacekeeping: Problems and Potential

Satish Nambiar

We are passing through a decisive stage in the history of the international system. Though the threat of war between great states or nuclear confrontation between major powers are well behind us and in fact fading in our memory, new and diverse forms of threats, some clear and present, others only dimly perceived, test our resolve and question the validity of our existing mechanisms. Developments at the international level over the last decade have exposed deep divisions within the membership of the United Nations over fundamental policies on peace and security. They have included debates on how best to prevent the proliferation of weapons of mass destruction, and combat the spread of international terrorism, the criteria for the use of force and the role of the Security Council, the effectiveness of unilateral versus multilateral responses to security, the notion of preventive war, and the place of the United Nations in a world with a single super power, whose position is being contested by an emerging power.

These debates emerge after several years of agonizing debate on issues of no less importance. Such as our collective response to civil wars; the effectiveness of existing mechanisms in responding to genocide; so-called ethnic cleansing and other severe violations of human rights; changing notions of state sovereignty; and the need to more tightly link the challenges of peace and the challenges of development. There is little doubt that aspects of restructuring and institutional reform of the UN machinery and its organs to meet the new challenges need to be addressed without further delay. The changes called for are not merely a matter of the functioning of the UN Secretariat and other such administrative details. The changes need to focus on the world body's character and ethos.

There is a unanimous view that meeting the challenges of today's threats means getting serious about prevention. Preventing wars within states and between them is in the collective interest of all of us. If the international community is to do better in the future in this context, the UN will need real improvements in its capacity for preventive diplomacy, mediation and conflict management.

The use of force should only be considered after all other options have been exhausted. And the fact that force can be legally used does not always mean that it should be used. The mechanism of preventive deployment is without doubt a most useful tool. Even so there can be little argument that prevention sometimes fails. And when that happens, threats will have to be met by military means. The UN Charter provides a clear framework for the use of force. States have an inherent right to self-defence, enshrined in Article 51. Long-established customary international law makes it clear that states can take military action as long as the threatened attack is imminent, no other means would deflect it, and the action is proportionate. Equally, Chapter VII of the UN Charter provides the international community represented by the Security Council, with the authority to deal with situations where military force needs to be applied against an errant state that resorts to aggression against another Member State. On preventive use of military force by Member States to deal with not-so-imminent threats, there is clearly a view that States that fear the emergence of distant threats have an obligation to bring such concerns to the notice of the Security Council for appropriate action. And there is general acceptance that on this specific aspect, the Security Council would need to be more pro-active than before.

The aspect of the responsibility of the international community to protect innocent civilians, who are victims of genocide or ethnic cleansing, is another sensitive one. In context of the fact that state sovereignty is still a very important issue for most developing countries that have emerged from colonial rule not too long back. Notwithstanding all the developments at the global level, the concept of state sovereignty remains at the root of the international system. Even so, there appears to be some consensus that in the twenty-first century such sovereignty cannot be absolute. The emerging norm of a collective responsibility to protect civilians from large-scale violence has been endorsed: a responsibility that lies first and foremost with national authorities. When a state fails to protect its civilians or is incapable of doing so, the international community would appear to have a responsibility to act, through humanitarian operations, monitoring missions, and diplomatic pressure; and with force if necessary as a very last resort. The reality, of course, is that the international community remains largely indifferent unless the vital interest of one or more of the important players is directly affected. Even when there is consensus that force has to be applied, resources are not always readily available or forthcoming.

Deploying military and police personnel for peacekeeping and enforcement action has proven to be a valuable tool in ending wars and helping to secure states in their aftermath. The demands for such deployment seem to be growing exponentially. From indications available today, just to do an adequate job of keeping the peace in existing conflicts may require almost doubling the number of peacekeepers around the world. Developed countries have particular responsibilities to do more to provide military and police personnel for deployment to UN peace operations. And if we are to meet the challenges ahead, Member States will have to be prepared to make available more trained military and civilian police personnel for UN purposes, together with appropriate equipment, air transport and other strategic lift capacities to assist peace operations. There is no greater legitimacy for the use of military forces, and for that matter, civilian police, than for the maintenance of international peace and security. It should therefore be a matter of honour and privilege for countries to provide forces for such peace missions.

In this context, however, the practical experience in this context is invariably rather dismal. The inordinate delay in the arrival of troops in the mission areas is always a most frustrating feature of the missions that are being set up. It is in recognition of this basic inadequacy that rapid deployment forces like the Nordic Sherbrig, the European Union Rapid Deployment Force, the proposed sub-regional rapid deployment capability of the African Union, and so on, have been, or are being, put in place. One of the measures instituted by the UN following the Brahimi Panel report in 2000 to overcome the shortcoming has been the earmarking of "stand by" forces by Member States. This is most commendable and needs full support. As on date, this arrangement apparently provides for over 100,000 personnel pledged by about 75 Member States. However, it is a moot point whether such "stand by" forces would in fact, be available immediately on demand. The Rwandan experience (and many others since), indicates that political expediency and domestic compulsions will invariably dictate the responses of Member States. Therefore, while this arrangement must stand, it would be pragmatic to work on the assumption that forces under this arrangement can only be put together in an extended time frame; possibly about three months or so; subject of course, to political acceptance by Member States. To expect forces any earlier is unrealistic under prevailing conditions.

There is little need to dwell at any great length on the point that a military force of modest dimensions (together with police and civil affairs and humanitarian aid personnel where necessary) inserted into a conflict zone as soon as some semblance of agreement between belligerents is negotiated, can achieve much more in terms of implementation of the terms of the agreement, than a much larger force introduced three to six months later. Given the fact that during such delay, the political situation within the mission area can change dramatically, hostilities could well have resumed, and the ground situation so much changed as to diminish the chances of peaceful resolution. If this is so clearly evident, it would appear that inhibitions about having a suitably organized, structured and equipped "standing force" that is readily available to the UN when required are somewhat misplaced.

Whereas this idea has been mooted in the past on several occasions including by veteran peacekeepers like former Under Secretary General in charge of peacekeeping, Sir Brian Urquhart, and there is general agreement to the concept in principle, a point often made in New York by those who do not favour such a proposal is that it is unlikely to receive the endorsement of Member States of the UN on grounds of costs of establishing and supporting such a force, as also on grounds of political acceptance of the idea. To the objective analyst these postulations seem quite unconvincing. In my view, reluctance to endorse such a concept particularly by the more powerful countries of the developed world, is primarily because they would not like to see their own influence and ability to manipulate events diluted by the provision of such ready capability to the United Nations. To that extent, much of the talk about strengthening the UN and making it more effective is largely rhetoric. The point is probably underscored by the fact that the developed world has shown increasing reluctance over the last few years to providing military personnel for UN peace operations particularly in difficult missions in Africa.

Governments of developed countries of the Western world seem to prefer making available their well-equipped and trained forces to NATO or EU sponsored interventions even in missions outside their area of operations, to complement UN operations rather than being part of such operations.

It would be useful to remind ourselves that crises in the twenty-first century are not likely to be only due to wars between states but more often than not, conflict generated by internal discord, terrorism and natural and manmade disasters. Even so, most nations and some regional organizations continue to equip themselves to deal with threats to national sovereignty if and when they arise. That will no doubt continue with more focus in some regions affected by disputes left behind by recent history as in the case of India's disputes with China and Pakistan. To that extent, notwithstanding the efforts by countries for acquisition and maintenance of military equipment for sub-conventional, conventional and even warfare under a nuclear overhang, there is a general awareness that wars between states are not the real threat today. The international community should be looking at measures for dealing with terrorism, internal conflict that also includes genocide, ethnic cleansing, war crimes and crimes against humanity, disaster relief, and so on under international oversight through UN peace operations, or regional initiatives.

The UN and other international organizations and military alliances like NATO were set up in the aftermath of the Second World War and structured to deal with inter-state conflict. But with the international community now wrestling with intra-state conflict situations and terrorist threats there is a need for fresh thinking and solutions. Traditional UN peacekeeping has served the international community well in the years past. It is an area in which India has considerable experience and expertise; having participated in 45 of the 66 UN peacekeeping operations since 1948 with over 120,000 personnel to date, including every operation in Africa, incurring over 135 fatalities in the process.

Large troop contributions in Gaza/Sinai (1956-1967), Congo (1960-1964), Angola (1995), Mozambique (1992-1993), Cambodia (1992-1994), Somalia (1994-1995), Rwanda (1994-1995), Sierra Leone (2000-2001), etc. With current deployment of over 8,000 in nine operations (including the Democratic Republic of Congo (DRC), Sudan, Lebanon), India is the third largest contributor today. Indian Air Force attack helicopters have been provided to the missions in the DRC and Sudan. Experienced police contributions have been made and continue to be made, to UN missions world-wide. Of particular significance is the deployment of an all-woman contingent in Liberia since the last six years.

Traditional methods and old tools are not effective or appropriate in today's intra-state conflict situations, where innocent civilians are being increasingly targeted. Furthermore, current operations are generally under-resourced and lack sustained political back-up support. UN establishment and troop contributors are trying to cope with calls for "robust" operations that entail use of force. The Department of Peacekeeping Operations at the UN headquarters in New York is trying to evolve concept and doctrine to meet these emerging demands.

This is an area in which EU and India could cooperate. But the reality is that Europe's participation in UN peacekeeping is marginal today. Hence trained forces and 'state-of-the-art' equipment that are available in the developed world are not being provided to the UN when they are most required. European countries prefer to make their forces and equipment available for the North Atlantic Treaty Organization (NATO) or EU-led combat operations. Though NATO is not a regional organization under the terms of Chapter VIII of the UN Charter, it has assumed a role for itself in the maintenance of peace and security within Europe and increasingly beyond its original area of operations. Thus, while the European Union can play a regional and global role in maintaining international peace and security, one cannot envisage India agreeing to be part of such an arrangement, unless there is endorsement by either the UN Security Council or the General Assembly and an appropriate international umbrella is set up.

I must express disappointment that despite the efforts we have made at various bilateral and multilateral forums, European countries and institutions dealing with the subject, have shown little interest in inter-acting or putting in place mechanisms for exchanging peacekeeping experiences and sharing conceptual thoughts on the subject with our Centre for United Nations Peacekeeping in New Delhi.

The armed forces of many European countries participated in the military operations in Afghanistan and Iraq, that later necessitated the conduct of counter-insurgency operations. Such operations continue in Afghanistan and it is not inconceivable that such commitments may well arise again in the future. Dealing with insurgency and terrorism is something the Indian Armed Forces have long been engaged with. Hence, this is a field of military activity that India can offer a great deal of expertise based on experience. And given the fact that such operations do not provide 'quick-fix' solutions, we in India can also learn from the EU experiences.

Finally, as we enter the second decade of the twenty-first century there is increasing focus on the protection of innocent civilians in conflict. The Outcome Document of the 2005 World Summit endorsed the UN Secretary General's recommendation on the "Responsibility to Protect" (RtoP). This was subsequently endorsed in the UN General Assembly in 2006 and most recently in July 2009. Notwithstanding the severe reservations in much of the developing world about this concept as being a "western" one aimed at intervention and regime change through the 'use of force', ignoring national sovereignty, there seems to be some effort to look at the concept more objectively. There is greater recognition that it is the responsibility of the State to protect its populations; and that when it is either unable or unwilling to fulfill this responsibility, the international community has a responsibility to step in to assist the State and support it in its attempts or coax it to do so by using all available means other than the use of force. In the extreme case where everything else fails, the international community through the medium of the UN Security Council and through the use of regional or global mechanisms may authorise the use of force, with great discrimination and with the responsibility to follow up with peace building to restore state authority, mechanisms and infrastructure. This may well be an area for more meaningful and useful future cooperation between the EU and India.

6

India-EU Broad-based Trade and Investment Agreement

Gulshan Sachdeva

With more than US$111 billion bilateral trade,[1] the European Union (EU) is India's largest trading partner. Foreign Direct Investment (FDI) in India from EU Member States is higher than investments from the United States and Japan put together. Similarly, Indian companies are also buying many European firms. Encouraged by these positive trends, India and the EU are negotiating for a Broad-Based Trade and Investment Agreement (BTIA) since 2007. These negotiations, however, have taken much longer than expected. Achieving this agreement has been one of the major targets of the Joint Action Plan launched under the India-EU Strategic Partnership. Despite many deadlines, however, the recurring postponement of the conclusion of the trade talks has become a regular feature of India-EU summits in the last few years. Is it the complexity of negotiations, particularly dealing with products like cars, wines, spirits, pharmaceuticals as well as services trade and procurement which are delaying the agreement? Or it is just a lack of imagination or political will from both sides in the current uncertain European economic climate and policy paralysis in India which is affecting a bilateral deal?

This chapter analyses how trade and economic ties have formed the core of India-EU relations. The global economic slowdown and continuing Eurozone crisis in the EU have also had an adverse effect on economic ties. The chapter argues that the main challenge facing policy-makers on both sides is to conclude a trade and investment agreement in an increasingly uncertain European economic climate as well as less favourable economic and political climate in India.

Background

In the last two decades, India's global vision of a democratic, multicultural and multipolar world coincides with that of Europe. Similarly, while a new economic and security architecture is evolving in Asia, Europe's engagement with Asia will be incomplete unless it partners India. Realizing the importance of this, the two entities instituted annual summit meetings (supplemented by business summits) in 2000. These meetings resulted in the India-EU Strategic Partnership (2004) and launched a Joint Action Plan in 2005 at the sixth summit in Delhi. In 2006, India was also invited to join the Asia-Europe Meeting (ASEM) – an informal process of dialogue between Asia and Europe.

Historically, trade and economic relations with Europe have always been important for India and formed the core of India-European Economic Community (EEC)/EU relations. Realising the importance of economic relations with European countries, India was among the first few countries to establish diplomatic relations with the EEC in 1962. Later bilateral agreements were signed in 1973 and 1981. In 1974, a comprehensive agreement was signed between India and the EEC which covered a wide range of economic issues covering trade, economic cooperation, industry, services, energy, telecommunication, tourism, private sector, investment, science and technology, intellectual property, agriculture, development cooperation, environment and human resource development.[2]

This was the first agreement signed by the EC with any non-associated developing country embodying the concepts of commercial and economic cooperation linked with trade. This agreement provides for a Joint Commission and three Sub-Commissions on trade and commercial cooperation, economic cooperation and development cooperation. Six working groups in the areas of agriculture and marine products, information technology, the environment, textiles, and consular issues were also set up. In 2001, India and the EU signed a science and technology agreement. To simplify customs procedures and develop trade facilitation actions in customs matters in accordance with international standards, both signed a Custom Cooperation Agreement in 2004.

At the very first annual summit (2000), India and the EU agreed to enhance trade and cooperation. The 11th EU Joint Commission encouraged industry to launch the Joint Initiative to Enhance Trade and Investment. Twelve summits have so far taken place with the last one in Delhi in February 2012. The agenda for these summits has been set by the prevailing economic, political and strategic environment. Major issues discussed during the last few summits include trade and economic issues, energy and climate change, the global economic situation and governance, and global and regional security issues, particularly Afghanistan.[3]

Trade Dynamics

At the start of the planning process in 1951, the share of the United Kingdom in India's total exports was about 24 per cent. Similarly, about 21 per cent of imports came from the UK. Another major trading partner was the United States. In the early 1960s, about 37 per cent of Indian trade was with Member States of the EEC with the UK and West Germany being major trade partners. Subsequently, trade with other countries, especially the Netherlands and Belgium became important. Thus, trade with the EC was an important component of Indian foreign economic relations in the 1960s and 1970s. Its relative importance, however, somewhat declined as India forged special trade and economic relations with the countries of the former Soviet bloc. In 1971, India was the first Asian country to which the EC granted the Generalised System of Preferences (GSP) facility, which sought to encourage exports of manufacturing goods of poor developing countries. Some studies have, however, concluded that owing to structural rigidities and the list of sensitive goods, the impact of the scheme has been marginal.[4]

In recent years, Indian exports to the EU-27 have increased from about US$8.8 billion in 1996-97 to about US$53 billion in 2011-12.[5] Similarly, India imported commodities worth US$58 billion in the same year from the EU. This was nearly a six-fold increase from imports of US$10.6 billion in 1996-97. Due to the global economic slowdown, bilateral trade declined to about $74 billion in 2009-10, with $36 billion in exports and $38 billion in imports. Bilateral trade, however, has recovered again in the last two years (see Figure 6.1).

Figure 6.1: India-EU Trade, 1996-97 to 2011-12

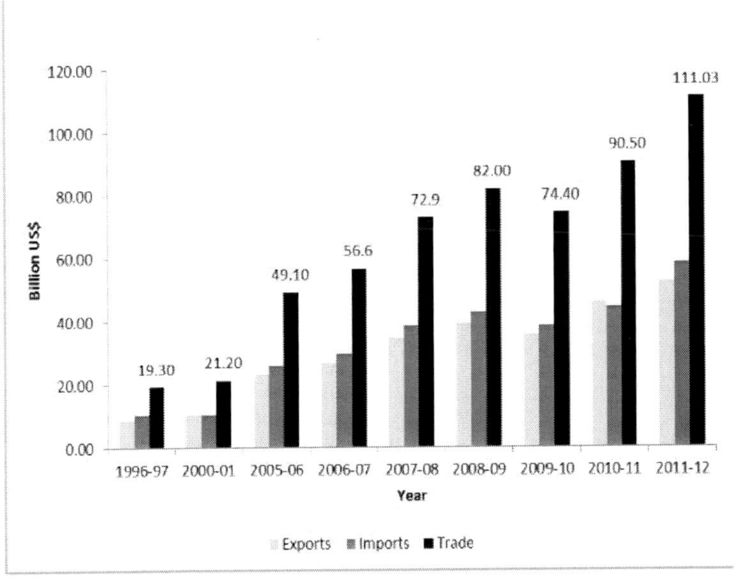

Source: Government of India, Ministry of Commerce and Industry.

India's major trading partners in the EU-27 are Germany, Belgium, the UK, the Netherlands, Italy, and France (Figure 6.2). In 2011-12, these six countries accounted for about 80 per cent of India's trade with the Union. The remaining 21 countries accounted for only 20 per cent of total trade with the EU-27. In recent years, imports from Sweden have witnessed a major spurt. For many years, the UK has been the major export market within the EU, accounting for 19 per cent of exports to the EU 27 and about 4 per cent of total Indian exports in 2007–08. In recent years, however, the Netherlands has become India's biggest export market within the EU.

Figure 6.2: India's Main Trading Partners in the EU, 2009-10 to 2011-12

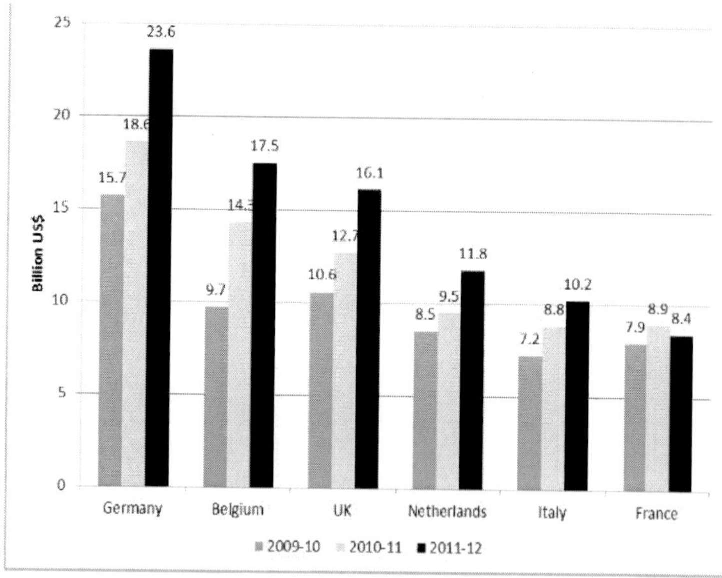

Source: *RBI Monthly Bulletin*, September 2012, pp. 1669 and 1671.

Although in absolute terms India's trade with the EU has increased, there are some disturbing trends. In relative terms as a percentage of India's total exports and imports, India-EU trade has declined consistently in the last decade or so. In 1996–

Table 6.1: EU Trade with Major Partners, 2011

Major Import Partners				*Major Export Partners*				*Major Trade Partners*			
Rank	*Partner*	*Million Euro*	*%*	*Rank*	*Partner*	*Million Eurc*	*%*	*Rank*	*Partner*	*Million Euro*	*%*
	Extra EU27	**1,683,931.0**	**100.0**		**Extra EU27**	**1,531,122.0**	**100.0**		**Extra EU27**	**3,215,053.0**	**100.0**
1	China	292,070.0	17.3	1	USA	260,566.8	17.0	1	USA	444,708.0	13.8
2	Russia	198,178.2	11.8	2	China	136,216.9	8.9	2	China	428,287.8	13.3
3	USA	184,141.2	10.9	3	Switzerland	121,690.6	7.9	3	Russia	306,627.1	9.5
4	Norway	93,528.7	5.6	4	Russia	108,448.9	7.1	4	Switzerland	212,894.7	6.6
5	Switzerland	91,204.1	5.4	5	Turkey	72,587.6	4.7	5	Norway	140,059.6	4.4
6	Japan	67,444.8	4.0	6	Japan	48,970.3	3.2	6	Turkey	120,176.0	3.7
7	Turkey	47,588.4	2.8	7	Norway	46,531.0	3.0	7	Japan	116,415.1	3.6
8	**India**	**39,256.9**	**2.3**	**8**	**India**	**40,419.4**	**2.6**	**8**	**India**	**79,678.2**	**2.5**

Source: Eurostat

97, India-EU-27 trade accounted for about 26.5 per cent of total Indian trade. However, in 2011-12, it declined to 13.9 per cent of total Indian trade (see Figure 6.3). In 2011-12, exports to the EU accounted for about 17.2 per cent of total Indian exports and imports from the EU accounted for about 11.9 per cent. In fact, growth rates of India-EU trade have not been similar to those of total Indian trade. Against an average of about 28.9 per cent growth of Indian trade in four years (between 2004-05 and 2007-08), India-EU trade grew at about 25.4 per cent. Similarly, compared to an average of about 34 per cent growth of Indian imports in these four years, imports from the EU grew at an average of about 26.5 per cent annually. This indicates that European economies have not been able to take full advantage of the rapid growth of the Indian economy.

Figure 6.3: India-EU Trade as a Percentage of Total Indian Trade

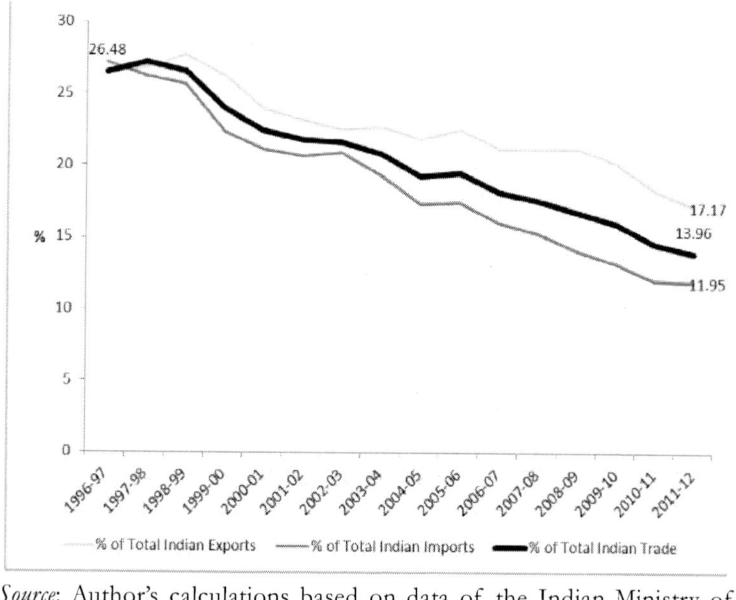

Source: Author's calculations based on data of the Indian Ministry of Commerce and Industry.

There was slightly better growth witnessed in Indo-US trade, which grew at an average rate of 26.3 per cent in these four years. China (bilateral trade grew at an average of 53 per cent annually in these four years) and member states of ASEAN were examples of countries which are integrating better with the Indian economy are. This explains why India is eager to sign trading arrangements with a number of Asian countries.

From the European perspective, India's importance has slightly increased in recent years. In 2011, India was EU's eight largest partner with 2.5 per cent share (Table 6.1). In fact, if we exclude countries like Norway, Switzerland and Turkey which are part of broader Customs Union with the Union, India was an important trading partner outside EU-27, behind the United States, China, Russia and Japan.

The product composition of the main items of India-EU trade shows that India exports a wide variety of products to the Union. Major export items are manufactured goods, readymade garments, gems and jewellery, pharmaceuticals, organic chemicals, leather goods, vehicles and machinery. The highest growth was witnessed in food items, iron and steel, etc. Major imports include gems and jewellery, machinery, electronic goods, chemicals, iron and steel, aluminium, etc. Similar items in both lists indicate that considerable intra-industry trade is also taking place. The product composition of trade in recent years reveals that bilateral trade in agricultural products is virtually negligible. Major items of trade are manufactured products, including machinery, transport equipment, etc. For many years, India had balance of trade problems with many EU countries. In the earlier decades, the trade debate in India was dominated by concern over balance-of-trade issues. However, with large foreign exchange reserves and high annual GDP growth rates, Indian foreign trade will continue to expand with relatively large trade deficits in the near future. Therefore, trade deficit, which influenced trade talks between India and Europe in the past, has ceased to be an important issue.

Table 6.2: EU Trade with India by SITC Section (2011)

SITC Codes	*SITC Sections*	*Value (mn Euros)*	*Share of Total (per cent)*	*Share of Total EU imports (per cent)*
	EU Imports from India			
	Total	**39,257**	**100**	**2.3**
SITC 6	Manufactured goods classified chiefly by material	9,572	24.4	5.2
SITC 8	Miscellaneous manufactured articles	8,524	21.7	4.0
SITC 7	Machinery and transport equipment	7,004	17.8	1.6
SITC 5	Chemicals and related products	5,125	13.1	3.4
SITC 3	Mineral fuels, lubricants and related materials	4,819	12.3	1.0
SITC 0	Food and live animals	2,131	5.4	2.5
SITC 2	Crude materials, inedible, except fuels	940	2.4	1.2
SITC 9	Commodities and transactions	622	1.6	2.1
SITC 4	Animal and vegetable oils, fats and waxes	266	0.7	3.1
SITC 1	Beverages and tobacco	168	0.4	2.4
	EU Exports to India			
	Total	**40,419**	**100**	**2.6**
SITC 7	Machinery and transport equipment	15,729	38.9	2.4
SITC 6	Manufactured goods classified chiefly by material	13,480	33.3	6.9
SITC 5	Chemicals and related products	4,225	10.5	1.7
SITC 8	Miscellaneous manufactured articles	2,665	6.6	1.7
SITC 2	Crude materials, inedible, except fuels	2,415	6.0	5.9
SITC 3	Mineral fuels, lubricants and related materials	307	0.8	0.3
SITC 9	Commodities and transactions	296	0.7	0.7
SITC 0	Food and live animals	234	0.6	0.4
SITC 1	Beverages and tobacco	87	0.2	0.3
SITC 4	Animal and vegetable oils, fats and waxes	22	0.1	0.6

Source: Eurostat

Table 6.3: EU27 Trade in Services with India (million Euros)

	Exports			*Imports*			*Balance*		
	2008	*2009*	*2010*	*2008*	*2009*	*2010*	*2008*	*2009*	*2010*
Total	**8,938**	**9,137**	**10,862**	**8,129**	**7,390**	**8,692**	**809**	**1,747**	**2,170**
of which:									
Transportation	2,850	2,391	3,577	1,821	1,488	1,835	1,029	903	1,742
Travel	1,018	874	1,230	2,017	1,470	1,660	-999	-597	-430
Other services	**5,069**	**5,968**	**6,052**	**4,282**	**4,425**	**5,182**	**788**	**1,442**	**870**
of which:									
Communications services	278	261	230	267	207	187	10	55	43
Construction services	322	487	481	132	224	204	190	253	277
Insurance services	73								
Financial services	350	322	310	80	133	187	270	189	123
Computer an information services	1,356	1,732	1,811	1,125	1,288	1,530	230	444	281
Royalties and license fees	212	247	258	50	29	49	162	218	219
Other business services	2,243	2,548	2,693	2,472	2,333	2,835	-229	215	-141
Personal cultural and recreational services	28	21	32	30	69	33	-2	-48	-0.2
Government services other	208	181	146	71	89	69	137	91	77
Total extra-EU27	525,304	483,493	539,028	454,045	416,271	453,604	71,259	67,222	85,424
India/total extra-EU27	1.7%	1.9%	2.0%	1.8%	1.9%				

Source: *EU India Summit*, Eurostat New Release 20/2012, 9 February 2012

Services Trade

Services are becoming increasingly important in India-EU trade. In fact, issues concerning services will determine the fate of bilateral negotiations on the Broad-Based Bilateral Trade and Investment Agreement. In 2008, the share of services (including construction) in the EU gross value added was 78.1 per cent. In the same year, services accounted for about 55 per cent of the Indian economy. The EU is the biggest global player in international trade in services. In 2008, the EU's international trade in services recorded a surplus of €75.4 billion. Its total trade in services was €965 billion (€520 billion exports and €445 billion imports). India is also becoming a significant player in global services trade. India's trade in services with the EU-27 grew from €7.8 billion in 2004 to about €17.9 billion in 2010. In recent years, India has recorded a surplus in travel, computer and information services and communication services. The total deficit recorded with the EU was about €1.4 billion in 2008 and €1.7 billion in 2010. For services export, the UK has been India's biggest market within the EU, followed by Germany and France.

Investment Linkages

Apart from trade in goods and services, the EU is also a major investor in India. The Union's share in India's total FDI approvals during January 1991 to December 2005 was around 25 per cent. These investment approvals rose from US$78 million in 1991 to US$2.314 billion in 2001. From 2001, there was a further increase in investments from the EU. Between April 2000 and June 2012, cumulative FDI inflow from the EU countries amounted to about US$ 43 billion which was about 25 per cent cent of total FDI inflows into India during this period. This was more than the combined American and Japanese FDI. During the same period, the UK was the EU's top investor in India, followed by the Netherlands, Cyprus, Germany and France. The problem with data about Indian FDI is that it is difficult to accurately trace country-wise data. Another difficulty is that a large amount of investments by European and American firms to India may be routed through Mauritius. Between April 2000 and June 2012, about 37 per cent of total FDI in India was reportedly from Mauritius. Similarly, investments from Cyprus is greater than Germany, France, Spain and Italy (see Table 6.4).

Table 6.4: FDI Inflows in India, April 2000 to June 2012 (US$ million)

Country	*FDI Inflows*	*Per cent of Total Inflows*
Mauritius	65,607	37.55
Singapore	17,555	10.05
Japan	12,663	7.25
USA	10,709	6.13
European Union	42,983	24.58
UK	16,313	9.33
Netherlands	7,652	4.37
Cyprus	6,602	3.78
Germany	4,880	2.79
France	2,988	1.71
Spain	1,157	0.66
Italy	1,107	0.63
Sweden	936	0.54
Belgium	466	0.27
Other EU Member States	882	0.50

Source: Government of India, Department of Industrial Policy and Promotion, FDI Statistics.

Although there is also significant variation among various Eurostat publications, the following table provides some trends from the organisation's latest reports.

Table 6.5 indicates that FDI has not been in one direction. Indian FDI in the EU soared to about €10 billion in 2007. Since then it has declined significantly. This suggests that negative economic news about the Eurozone economy has had an adverse affect on Indian investments in the EU. According to some estimates, between 2000 and 2007, around 900 Indian companies invested about $12 billion in EU Member States.

Table 6.5: FDI flows between India and the EU, 2001-10 (in million Euros)

Year	*EU FDI in India*	*Indian FDI in EU*
2001	348	108
2002	1,074	133
2003	747	614
2004	1,562	0
2005	2,546	548
2006	2,390	879
2007	4,019	10,118
2008	3,272	2,560
2009	3,207	800
2010	4,700	500

Source: Complied from various Eurostat publications.

Table 6.6: Indian FDI in EU, 1990-2007 (million US$)

	1990-97	*2000-2007*	*Number of Investing Firms*
European Union	**1,021**	**12,061**	**857**
Austria	37	5	12
Belgium and Luxembourg	17	187	41
Cyprus	20	1,359	36
Czech Republic	1	35	5
Denmark		27	5
Finland	2	-	4
France	3	109	28
Germany	24	138	131
Greece	3	-	2
Hungary	3	2	9
Ireland	38	13	13
Italy	42	54	16
Latvia	1		2
Malta		64	1
Netherlands		1,701	79
Poland	1	2	9
Spain	1	13	10
Sweden	3	10	8
UK	798	8,353	531

Source: Jaya Prakash Pradhan, *India's Emerging Multinationals in the Developed Region*, Munich Personal RePEc Archive Paper No. 12361, p. 5.

This constituted about 76 per cent of Indian greenfield investments abroad in developed countries. The UK has been a major attraction for Indian companies with more than 500 Indian companies investing around $9 billion between 1990 and 2007. The Netherlands and Cyprus are other main destinations. The majority of earlier investments in the UK have been in the service sector. In recent years, there have been major investments in the manufacturing sector as well.[6]

Apart from greenfield investments, Indian companies have been actively involved in overseas acquisitions. According to some estimates, 306 Indian firms were involved in 596 acquisitions worth $47 billion between 2000 and 2008 in the developed world. Out of these acquisitions, European deals represented more than 50 per cent in value terms.

Table 6.7: Overseas Acquisitions by Indian Firms in the EU, 2000-08 (million US$)

Region/Country	*Value*
European Union	**23,536**
Austria	133
Belgium	910
Czech Republic	43
Denmark	16
Finland	101
France	316
Germany	3,115
Greece	16
Hungary	44
Ireland	169
Italy	363
Netherlands	486
Poland	8
Portugal	69
Spain	173
Sweden	87
UK	17,488

Source: Jaya Prakash Pradhan, *India's Emerging Multinationals in the Developed Region* Munich Personal RePEc Archive Paper No. 12361, p. 14.

Technical and Financial Collaborations

The EU is also one of the major sources of technology transfer to India. During the period between August 1991 and December 2004, Indian authorities approved more than 3,600 technical collaborations from the EU-25 countries, which accounted for about 38 per cent of total technical collaborations during this period. The highest number of technical collaborations was in the area of electrical equipment (including computer software), industrial machinery and chemicals. Germany has emerged as a clear leader in technical collaboration from the EU with about 1,088 technical collaborations. The UK and Italy were in the second and third place respectively with 843 and 473 approved collaborations. In the area of financial collaborations, the UK is the leader with more than 1,600 collaborations. The total number of technical and financial collaborations signed between Indian and companies based in the Union between 1991 and 2004 is 9,745, was about 37 per cent of total collaborations signed by Indian companies. In comparison, about 6,080 financial and technical collaborations were approved with American companies. According to the Indo-German Chamber of Commerce, the Indo-German collaboration companies were market leaders in as many as fifteen product groups.

India-EU BTIA: A Status Report

New thinking on India-EU economic relations has been fostered by some of the above-mentioned factors. However, other factors have had an adverse influence on trade negotiations. The collapse of the Doha development round of WTO negotiations has pushed many countries, including India, to look for alternatives to multilateral negotiations to enhance foreign trade. In recent years, India has put its proposed regional trade agreements on the fast track. In the past, India had adopted a cautious approach to regionalism, and was engaged in only a few bilateral/regional initiatives, mainly through Preferential Trade Agreements (PTAs) or through open regionalism. In recent years, however, it has started concluding Comprehensive Economic Cooperation Agreements (CECAs) with many countries. These CECAs encompass a FTA in goods (zero customs duty regime within a fixed time frame on items covering substantial trade, and a relatively small negative list of sensitive items with no or limited duty concessions), services, investment and identified areas of economic cooperation. Such agreements include the South Asian Free Trade Area (SAFTA), the India-ASEAN agreement, Framework Agreement for India-BIMSTEC FTA, India-Thailand FTA, India-Singapore CECA, the India-South Korea agreement, etc. India already had FTAs with Sri Lanka and Nepal.

In 2011, India also signed a trade agreement with Japan – its first agreement with a developed country. The Indo-Japan FTA covers more than 90 per cent of trade, a vast gamut of services, investment, intellectual property rights, customs and other trade-related issues. India has pledged to reduce more than 90 per cent of its tariffs over a ten-year period. Japan has eliminated duties on 87 per cent of its tariff lines with the immediate reduction of tariffs to zero.[7]

A trade and investment deal is also being negotiated with the Gulf Cooperation Council (GCC), MERCOSUR, South Korea, Chile, etc. India-Israel, India-Brazil, South Africa (IBSA) and India-Russia joint study groups for concluding a FTA have also been set up. Within this broader context, attempts to finalise India-EU broad based agreement are also underway.

On the recommendations of the High Level Trade Group (HLTG), which was set up under the Joint Action Plan in 2005, it was agreed at the seventh summit in 2006 at Helsinki that both sides move towards negotiation for a broad-based trade and investment agreement. Both sides agreed that negotiations could begin on the following issues:

(*a*) *Trade in Goods:* (i) achieving elimination of duties on 90 per cent of tariff lines and trade volume within seven years of the entry into force of the agreement; (ii) modalities for the treatment of sensitive products including review clauses and partial liberalisation.

(*b*) *Trade in Services:* (i) ensure substantial sectoral coverage measured in terms of number of sectors, volume of trade and modes of supply. No mode of supply should be excluded; and (ii) provide for the elimination of substantially all discrimination between the parties.

(*c*) *Investment:* (i) improve market access and provide for national treatment to investors; (ii) ensure that host and home states retain their right to regulate; (iii) foster transparency by clarifying the regulatory framework; (iv) aim at freeing the flow of payments and investment-related capital movements; and (v) seek to facilitate the movement of investment-related natural persons.

(*d*) *Public Procurement:* Competitive Procurement Regime.

(*e*) *Technical Regulations:* Cooperation on Technical Barriers to Trade (TBT) and Sanitary and Phyto-Sanitary Measures (SPS).

(*f*) *Intellectual Property* (IP) and Geographical Indicators (GIs) coverage to IP and GIs in any future agreement.

(*g*) *Competition Policy:* Agreement on framework in any future agreement.

(*h*) *Dispute settlement* (DS) and provision of DS mechanism.

It is clear from the agenda that India and Europe are aiming at not just a simple free-trade agreement but a much larger pact which includes services, intellectual property, public procurement, competition policy, etc. In the beginning, both sides were more ambitious. It is now being realised, however, that it was perhaps better to "do the doable" first and go for comprehensive agreement later.[8]

Despite the environment being conducive to a trade deal, governments on both sides have been remarkably slow in negotiations: three deadlines have already been missed and more than a dozen rounds of negotiations have taken place alternatively in Brussels and Delhi. The fourteenth round of negotiations was held in Delhi in December 2011. At the ninth India-EU summit in France in 2008, leaders agreed to conclude the agreement by 2009 and double their trade in five years.[9] At the eleventh summit in Brussels, both sides fixed a mid-2011 deadline to conclude negotiations. After missing another deadline, the twelfth in Delhi in February 2102 reiterated that "negotiations on an ambitious and balanced package are now close to completion" and both sides would "monitor the progress of these negotiations for an early conclusion."[10]

The Federation of Indian Chambers and Commerce and Industry (FICCI) has expressed concerns that all items of export interest to India, like leather, textiles and garments, may not get covered under the FTA being negotiated with the EU. It suggested the expansion of scope of the pact to cover 95 per cent of merchandise goods.[11] The Communist Party of India (Marxist) asserts that unless details of the agreement are discussed by the Indian Parliament, no commitments should be made. The Politbureau of the Party warns that "such FTAs can turn out to be much more damaging for the livelihoods of our farmers, workers and other sections of the working people than the WTO agreements."[12] Already a campaign group led by trade unions and non-profit organisations have asked the government to halt the talks.[13] A serious campaign has argued that the proposed India-EU FTA would stop the flow of cheap drugs to the developing world.[14] Similarly, the domestic industry lobby, the Society of Indian Automobile Manufacturers (SIAM), argues that the proposed deal would kill investments and technology inflow and jeopardise the targets set under the government's own Automotive Mission Plan.[15] Therefore, some domestic opposition, the difficult global economic situation and developments on other bilateral economic pacts have already affected India-EU FTA negatively.

Some academic studies have looked at the implications of

a possible EU-India trade and investment pact. A joint study by Consumer Unity and Trusts Society (CUTS) India and Sussex University asserts that instead of shallow integration (the removal of border barriers to trade, typically tariffs and quotas), it would be far more effective if the EU and India go for deeper integration (which involves policies and institutions that facilitate trade by reducing or eliminating regulatory and behind-the-border impediments to trade).These policies could include issues such as customs procedures, regulation of domestic services production that discriminate against foreigners, product standards that differ from international norms or where testing and certification of foreign goods is complex and perhaps exclusionary, regulation of inward investments, competition policy, intellectual policy protection and the rules surrounding access to government procurement.[16] The study also suggests that an EU-India FTA is likely to increase FDI flows from the EU by 27 per cent and FDI stocks by 18 per cent. Another report by Decreux and Mitaritonne argues that the impact of the pact would be positive for both the partners. However, in India's case strong positive results will arise only in areas where there is a sufficient level of liberalisation in services.[17]

The Eurozone Crisis and India-EU Economic Ties

India-EU economic relations have also been greatly influenced by internal European economic developments. In the last two decades, the process of European economic integration has undergone tremendous changes. The establishment of the Economic and Monetary Union (EMU), the arrival of the Euro as well as enlargement of the EU to 28 Member States was best viewed in the context of its overall trends towards globalisation. The advent of the Euro also completed the Single Market, which had already ensured the free movement of goods, services, people and capital in the EU. After its successful launch in 1999, the Euro also became the most tangible symbol of a common 'European identity'. It also strengthened the image of Europe worldwide. After decades of success, however, many Eurozone economies are discovering that a single monetary policy in the absence of a single fiscal policy is not working. Despite promises of static and dynamic efficiency gains as a result of a single currency, the Eurozone's economic performance in the last decade has been relatively slow.

After an impressive performance in the last decade, many 'peripheral' economies in the Eurozone are facing a serious debt crisis. The European sovereign debt crisis has grown into one of the biggest challenges the EU has faced in recent times. After Greece, Portugal and Ireland, Italy and Spain are also showing dangerous signs of financial and economic instability. To tackle the issue, the European political elite have initiated several unprecedented measures. Along with the IMF, Eurozone Member States provided financial support to affected countries in the form of pooled bilateral loans. This included a €120 billion package to Greece; €85 billion assistance to Ireland; and €78 billion financing for Portugal. A second bailout package for Greece worth €109 billion has also been agreed upon with easier repayment terms from the private lenders. In so doing, the EU has effectively abandoned the 'no bailout' clause of the Lisbon Treaty. They also first established the €440 billion European Financial Stability Fund (EFSF) and then expanded it into a €780 billion EFSF. Its mandate is to raise funds in capital markets to provide loans to Euro area Member States which are experiencing difficulty in obtaining financing at reasonable rates. The EFSF may also intervene in the primary debt market. To strengthen economic policy coordination in the Euro area, Member States have also agreed to a European semester and the Euro-Plus Pact. They have further decided to establish a permanent crisis-resolution mechanism, the European Stability Mechanism (ESM), in order to safeguard the Euro and financial stability in Europe. The ESM will build on the existing EFSM by mid-2013. There are also discussions about the creation of common Eurobonds backed by all 17 Eurozone countries.

Despite all these measures, the situation remains murky. European attempts to run a common monetary policy without a single fiscal policy is not working. There are reports of the possibility of Greece's exit from the Eurozone. The Euro may not collapse but there is a serious possibility of a Eurozone break-up, with one or more countries voluntarily abandoning the single currency or forced to exit. Already the European Council has agreed to amend the Lisbon Treaty to provide a legal basis for a permanent mechanism to resolve the Eurozone sovereign debt crisis. Now European policy-makers are working on a long-term plan to establish a European system to guarantee bank deposits, a Banking Union, fiscal integration, and common Eurobonds. The President of the European Central Bank (ECB), Mario Draghi, has declared that the ECB would do "whatever it takes to save the Euro".[18] Under its new plan, the Outright Monetary Transactions (OMT) scheme, the ECB has pledged to buy unlimited quantities of debt of up to three years in maturity. To qualify, a country would have to accept associated conditions, i.e. promise to make certain economic reforms.

Despite these measures, soon the EU might face a situation where a country leaves or is forced to leave the Economic and Monetary Union. This is going to be a highly challenging situation for the EU, both legally and practically. ECB studies have shown that while negotiated withdrawal would perhaps be possible, unilateral withdrawal will be highly controversial and forced expulsion would be almost impossible. The global economic slowdown as well as the crisis in the Eurozone has definitely affected India-EU trade and investment relations. Trade ties have not affected much as Germany, the biggest economy in the EU and India's largest trade partner in Europe has been doing relatively well. Nevertheless, there has been significant decline in Indian investments to Europe in the last three years.

Conclusion

For several decades, trade and economic relations with Europe have been very important for India. Since the early 1990s, the process of European economic integration and the process of economic liberalisation in India have created new opportunities both for Europe and India. However, the growth of India-EU trade has not been replicated the overall growth of total Indian trade. An important reason for this has been the slow growth of European economies in the last decade. In the last decade, Europe has also become an important destination for cross-border investments and overseas acquisitions by Indian companies. Although from the European point of view, India still accounts for a very small share in trade and investment, its importance is increasing significantly. EU companies want to engage with the rapidly growing Indian economy in a much more systematic manner. These factors have led to the start of negotiations for a future wide-ranging trade and investment agreement. This also fits well within the current series of FTA/ CECA agreements India has signed with many countries. Despite, compelling reasons for a broad based deal, negotiations have been extremely slow. The global slowdown in recent years also affected these talks negatively. In the last three years, the Eurozone sovereign debt crisis has further increased uncertainty in the EU economy. In these circumstances, the major challenge facing policy makers is to conclude negotiations before the thirteenth India-EU summit in 2013. Both sides were hopeful that they would be able to conclude the agreement by the end of 2013. For this to happen, however, strong political will is needed from both sides since on balance, both India and the EU stand to gain much more from the agreement than they stand to lose. In fact, the trade deal has turned into a litmus test for the commitment of both sides to the strategic partnership.[19] Therefore, early conclusion of a Broad-based Trade and Investment Agreement is likely to improve prospects of cooperation in other political and strategic issues as well.

Despite objections from certain sectors from both sides, policy-makers from both sides have openly declared their commitment to a deal. Most of the sensitive issues concerning banking, insurance, agriculture, human rights, labour standards and environmental issues have been tackled in mature manner.

It is hoped that both will be able to conclude a deal on the agreed areas before the next summit. Although both India and the European Union can wait for a proper agreement on intellectual property rights, competition policy and procurement, it would be necessary to find some common ground on services soon. If an agreement is not reached on at least goods and services by the next summit, the issue of India-EU BTIA may go into hibernation for several years.

NOTES

1 According to the Ministry of Commerce, Government of India's Export Import Databank, India-EU bilateral trade in 2011-12 was US$111,031 million.

2 For details see *Cooperation Agreement between the European Communities and the Republic of India on Partnership and Development*, available at: http://europa.eu.int/comm/external_relations/india/intro/agree08_94.pdf.

3 For details of all 12 summits and related documents, see http://eeas.europa.eu/delegations/india/eu_india/political_relations/strategic_partnership/index_en.htm.

4 Swapan K. Bhattacharya, *India and the European Union: Trade and Non-Tariff Barriers* (New Delhi: Aakar Books, 2005).

5 Unless otherwise indicated, all figures used in this article are from various publications of the Indian Ministry of Commerce and Industry and the Reserve Bank of India.

6 For details, see Jaya Prakash Pradan, *India's Emerging Multinationals in the Developed Region* (New Delhi: Institute for Studies in Industrial Development, 2008).

7 "India Japan Sign Free Trade Agreement," *Times of India*, 16 February 2011, at http://timesofindia.indiatimes.com/india/India-Japan-sign-free-trade-agreement/articleshow/7506864.cms.

8 Suman Modwel and Surendra Singh, "The EU-India FTA Negotiations:

Leading to an Agreement or Disagreement," *ORF Occasional Paper No. 32, February 2012* (New Delhi: Observer Research Foundation).

9 "India EU Set to Ink Trade Pact by 2009, Set 100 Bn Euro Target," *The Economic Times*, 28 September 2008. Available at: http://economictimes.indiatimes.com/News/Economy/Foreign_Trade/India-EU_to_ink_trade_pact_by_2009_set_100_bl_Euro_target/articleshow/3541388.cms.

10 India-EU Joint Statement, 10 February 2012, http://eeas.europa.eu/india/sum02_12/docs/20120210_joint_statement_en.pdf

11 "FTA with EU Must Cover 95 per cent Goods for Real Benefit to India," *Business Line*, 26 September 2008. Available at: http://www.thehindubusinessline.com/blnus/14261831.htm.

12 See Press Statement by the Politburo of the Communist Party of India (Marxist) on the proposed India-EU Free Trade Agreement, at http://cpim.org/statement/2008/09272008-india-eu%20fta.htm.

13 "Amid Protests, EU-India Talks begins today," available at http://www.livemint.com/2009/03/16222358/Amid-protests-EUIndia-trade.html.

14 Sarah Boseley, "Does EU/India Free Trade Agreement Spell the End of Cheap Drugs for Poor Countries?" *The Guardian,* 10 February 2012.

15 Pankaj Doval, "Auto Industry Against Inclusion in India-European Union Free Trade Agreement," *The Times of India,* 16 May 2012.

16 Michael Gasoriek et al, *Qualitative Analysis of a Potential Free Trade Agreement between the European Union and India* (Sussex: Centre for the Analysis of Regional Integration and Jaipur: CUTS International, 2007).

17 Yvan Decreux and Christina Mitoritonne, *Economic Impact of a Potential Free Trade Agreement Between the European Union and India* (Paris: CEPII-CERAM, 2007).

18 "Debt Crisis: Mario Draghi Pledges to do 'whatever it takes' to Save Euro," *The Telegraph*, 26 July 2012, at http://www.telegraph.co.uk/finance/financialcrisis/9428894/Debt-crisis-Mario-Draghi-pledges-to-do-whatever-it-takes-to-save-euro.html.

19 Bernd von Muenchow-Pohl, *India and the Europe in a Multipolar World* (Washington: Carnegie Endowment for International Peace, 2012).

7

EU Development Cooperation with India

Jayaraj Amin

The development policy of the European Economic Community (EEC) was launched soon after its establishment. It has become important both as 'its own' policy area and as a means of structuring the Community's relations with non-European, especially developing countries. Past colonial links determined the initial focus of the Community's development policy on the countries of sub-Saharan Africa, Caribbean and the Pacific (ACP) which were associated with the EEC (under Articles 131 and 136, Part IV of Rome Treaty), which entitled them to receive technical and financial aid as well as reductions in duty through the specially created European Development Fund (EDF).[1] This association was formalized in Yaounde-I (1963) and Yaounde-II (1969) conventions between eighteen ACP countries and six European countries. The scope and reach of the Union's development policy was expanded under the Maastricht Treaty on European Union (1992), which was accorded a legal status. It introduced three principles to improve the effectiveness of the policy, viz. complementarity (of Member States' policies, programmes and EC action), coordination (between two or more development partners and policies), and coherence (operation without contradiction in policies and programmes).[2]

The EU's development policy is today closely aligned with its trade policy. It encompasses aid, trade and humanitarian assistance. Article 177 of the Maastricht Treaty outlines the objectives of development policy, viz. develop and consolidate democracy and the rule of law, foster "sustainable economic and social development", "smooth and gradual integration into world economy", and support "the campaign against poverty".[3] The emphasis on the eradication of poverty was reiterated in the Union's support for and incorporation of the Millennium Development Goals (MDGs) (adopted by the United Nations General Assembly in 2000) in its own developmental policy. The Lisbon Treaty (2009) recognized the competence of the Union in the area of development cooperation[4] (Article 188 D, Para 1 and 2) and endorsed the goal of poverty eradication in development cooperation.[5]

Institutional Framework

The Development Cooperation Instrument (DCI), adopted in 2006 and launched in January 2007, serves as the legal framework for the EU's development cooperation with Asian and Latin American countries. The DCI replaces a wide range of earlier geographic and thematic instruments. It enumerates the various programmes that are eligible for cooperation, including poverty eradication and achievement of MDGs; basis needs (primary education and health); social cohesion and employment; governance, democracy, human rights and institutional reforms; trade and regional integration; sustainable development through environmental protection; sustainable integrated water resource management and fostering greater use of sustainable energy technologies, developing infrastructure and an increased use of information and communication technologies; sustainable rural development and ensuring food security; and assistance in post-crisis situations and fragile states.[6] The geographic orientation is supplemented by the thematic programmes of the DCI that include the "Investing in People" programme which supports, among others, good health for all, education, knowledge and skills (vocational), gender equality and other aspects of human and social development (including employment and social cohesion), children and youth as well as culture.[7]

Since 2007, the EU has initiated a "Country Strategy Paper" (CSP) for a period of five years in order to ensure better delivery and targeted development assistance. The CSP analyses the socio-economic and political situation in each country, outlines the objectives of development cooperation, and specifies an action plan.[8] This is complemented by a Multi-Annual National Indicative Programme (MIP) that outlines the priority areas and financial allocation. The MIP, in turn, leads to Annual Action Programmes, which specifies the objectives, assesses the implementation of programmes, and makes financial allocation. To that end, the Union adopts different policy frameworks depending on the situation in the target country.

The policy frameworks and agreements outlined above are not exclusive and may overlap. Brussels has also been keen to improve the strategic coherence between its aid, trade and development policy. It regards a democratic political system with liberal values to be a prerequisite for economic progress. The "European Consensus on Development" (2005) specifies that sustainable development includes good governance, human rights as well as political, economic, social and environmental aspects (clause 7). To that end, it pledges its support to national strategies.[9] The DCI too focuses on these priority areas. Thus, both instruments facilitate "structural reforms" in the target country in conformity with the general political and economic preferences of EU.

Since the 1990s, the EU has signed a number of 'new generation agreements' with many developing countries, which contain provisions on human rights, democratic principles, labour standards as well as good governance. The Union has even introduced a novel "GSP-Plus" scheme to support "sustainable development and good governance" if a "vulnerable" country has signed sixteen human rights conventions and at least seven (out of eleven) conventions on environment and governance.[10] The Cotonou Agreement stipulates that development cooperation seeks to establish a comprehensive partnership, "based on three complementary pillars of development cooperation, economic and trade cooperation and the political dimension".[11]

Trends in EU Development Cooperation Policy

The brief review of development cooperation suggests certain broad trends in the EU's development cooperation policy. *Firstly,* EU developmental policy is guided by economic considerations as well as political objectives. "Economic cooperation" is the new buzzword for the new type of development aid. It seeks to create a favourable macroeconomic and political milieu in the recipient countries through trade and investment. Aid agreements provide economic leverage to compel recipients to comply with the Union's political preferences and values like human rights.

Secondly, the EU increasingly prefers to align with the recipient's national development strategies rather than directly aiding the project in order to enhance the impact of sectoral management and foster an overall change in the priorities and operation. This shift from a project to a sector specific approach, in which structural reforms are seen as imperative, is complemented by "donor coordination" (both at the European level and with global institutions operating with broad similar objectives such as the International Monetary Fund (IMF) and the World Bank) and also by framing of "indicative" five-year programmes for the target country which outline objectives, establish long-term priorities and seek consistency in the Community assistance. These aspects were reiterated in the Lisbon Treaty.[12]

Thirdly, the EU is increasingly keen to conclude bilateral agreements notwithstanding its regional and global policies and strategies since they enable it to negotiate and better enforce its preferences than at the global level. The EU also regards trade and development goals to be linked and the market mechanism is seen as being conducive to development and, therefore, to multilateralism.

Fourthly, there is a marked emphasis on 'dialogues' as a means to structure development cooperation in the backdrop of market mechanism and its preferred political values. Since dialogues visualise the final beneficiaries of the programme, the EU prefers the involvement of an increasing number of NGOs and civil society actors in the process. This gives rise to an increased number of stakeholders in EU-recipient country relations. This also fits in well with its objectives for wider participation and involvement of people in developmental activity. This contributes to better implementation and fosters good governance – the main component of EU's development strategy.

Fifthly, 'reciprocity' has more or less has become the order of the day and unilateral concessions are almost becoming the events of the past. The emphasis now is on capacity building, regulatory mechanisms and 'Aid for Trade' (AfT) policy in order to increase trade policy capacity of developing countries, which include the Union's preferred values.[13] Thus, the EU is gradually moving away from the GSP scheme based on 'special and differential treatment' under the General Agreement on Tariffs and Trade (GATT)/World Trade Organisation (WTO) rules under 'objective criteria' like the level of development. This is evident in the ACP-EC-Partnership Agreement or Cotonou Agreement (2000). Even when concessions are given, e.g. under the 'Everything but Arms' (EBA) providing duty-free and quota-free access for LDCs exports into the EU market, the net benefit may be minimal since it tends to be nullified by EU's counter measures like exceptions, non-tariff barriers

(NTBs), 'sensitive products' (e.g. sugar, rice and bananas initially were not allowed under EBA), etc.

EU-India Development Cooperation: Background

The initial focus of EEC development policy was on Africa. With the approval of the Food Aid Convention (1967) by the Community, Asian and Latin American countries became the beneficiaries of EEC food aid. India. From 1968-1969 to 1970-1971, India received 80,000 tonnes of cereals out of the total 991,040 tonnes[14] whereas Pakistan received 165, 000 tonnes of food aid. During 1970-1974, India was the highest recipient of EEC food aid. It received 6.5 per cent of the total aid committed closely followed by Bangladesh with 6.4 per cent.[15] In 1976, the Union provided about €6 million to India as flood relief for Uttar Pradesh and Gujarat.

The General System of Preferences (1971) became the framework for EC's trade relationship with most developing countries including India. The first agreement with India was signed in December 1973 that stressed on development and expansion of commercial linkages. The agreement later paved the way for a broader agreement on Commercial and Economic Cooperation in June 1981 moving beyond mere trade issues. Initially, the EC extended humanitarian assistance and economic aid without expectations of behavioural change. The Cold War did not significantly influence the Community's policy towards India despite its close relations with the Soviet Union.

The adoption of the Single European Act, the end of the Cold War, the failure of socialism, and the widespread globalisation in the 1990s led to a significant change in the Union's attitude towards other regions. Brussels became increasingly determined to have its influence in the world and safeguard its economic interests. The new emphasis on the market as the driver of growth and neo-liberal policies that allowed more space to market forces with a minimum role to the state were generally supported by Western countries as well as by the IMF and World Bank. The realignment of the Union's policies with those of the Brettonwoods institutions and key Member States led the EU to enhance its global presence and promote governance and conflict resolution in its external policies and perspectives towards third countries with a renewed emphasis on the market economy and liberal values. To that end, a regulatory mechanism and rule-based effective multilateralism were deemed necessary. Brussels began to adopt a focused and long-term perspective incorporating 'European values' instead of ad hoc positions. EU development cooperation began to focus on structural reforms, market economy, reciprocal arrangements and multilateralism. The Council regulations (25 February 1992) on financial and technical assistance and economic cooperation with Latin American and Asian countries emphasized human rights, democratisation, good governance, and trade liberalisation.[16] This was well articulated in EU's "Towards a New Asia Strategy" (1994) which advocated a proactive policy towards the region and help integrate it into the open, market-based world trading system.[17]

Major Focus of EU-India Development Cooperation

EU-India development cooperation addresses diverse areas such as environment, gender, health, human rights, good governance, mutual awareness programmes and other areas of common interest including educational, scientific and cultural exchanges. Partnership programmes with important countries, in fact, are the means to identify or promote sectors and issues of common interest and are useful tools in shaping global order and multilateralism and promoting the values that the EU cherishes. The logic of openness and its contribution to the European growth and jobs is well articulated in the *2006 Global Europe Strategy* that sought to reorient bilateral trade agreements through a new generation of Free Trade Agreements (FTA) with focus on intellectual property and access to raw materials.[18]

India was becoming both a donor (under the "Indian Development and Economic Assistance Scheme – IDEAS") as well as a recipient of developmental assistance.

Given India's economic progress, the *Country Strategy Paper, India (2007-2013)* hoped that India's need for development assistance would gradually decline and that it would move towards support to pro-poor sector reform policies and other areas of mutual interest, including economic cooperation.[19] Thus, developmental assistance would be replaced by developmental cooperation, which was evident from the growth of joint programmes complementing Indian efforts. The CSP stressed the deepening of structural reforms (including better governance and infrastructure in order to improve investment climate, boost productivity and accelerate growth) and social cohesion (inclusive development). The CSP provided budgetary support to the social sector (health and education) encompassing best practice models in good governance, decentralised decision-making and development, gender issues, institutional reforms and public sector management in order to meet the MDGs apart from support for economic, academic, civil society and cultural activities foreseen in the Joint Action Plan (2005).[20] In order to realise the Millennium Development Goals, the EU pledged support for economic cooperation and sectoral/regulatory convergence. For instance, the EU had actively supported sectoral reform when the Government of India initiated the Health and Family Welfare Sector Investment Programme (SIP) in October 1998. The Union had earlier supported the District Primary Education Programme (DPEP) targeting districts with low female literary rates and the Sector Investment Programme (SIP). Brussels had also financed many rural development and natural resource management projects. However, the multiplicity and geographical dispersion of projects had limited and localised impact with little influence over long-term institution-building and policy.[21] Brussels has thus clearly moved away from project specific to sectoral priorities and reforms and synchronisation of development cooperation policies with other donors. Thus, in the case of the Sarva Siksha Abhiyan (SSA) (Education for All Movement), it cooperated with the World Bank and the British Department for International Development (DFID).

The EU has sought to support two priority areas, viz. social sectors (health and education) as well as economic, academic, civil society and cultural activities foreseen in the Joint Action Plan (JAP) (2005), revised in 2008.[22] In the social sector (primarily health and education), the Union sought to supplement two key Indian programmes, viz. Sarva Shiksha Abhiyan and the National Rural Health Mission (NRHM).[23] The former sought to achieve the universalisation of elementary education whereas the latter forcused on basic health care delivery system targeting reduction in infant and maternal mortality ratio. In both these programmes, apart from the programme objectives, the emphasis is on capacity building, inclusiveness and involvement of civil society players. To that end, in the Multiannual Indicative Programme (MIP-I) (2007-2010), the EU allocated €70 million for education, €110 million for the health sector and €80 million for the Joint Action Plan (JAP). In the MIP-II (2011-2013), €100-130 million, €50 million and €30-60 were earmarked for education, health and JAP initiatives respectively.[24]

Other activities supported by the EU are economic sectoral dialogues and cooperation (in trade, energy, science and technology, customs cooperation, etc.), civil society and cultural exchanges, academic exchanges (including cooperation in the higher education sector and EU and Indian Studies Centres). Furthermore, policy dialogues and sectoral actions are envisaged for a wide range of areas where the two sides have jointly identified a scope for enhanced cooperation leading to better governance and policy-making (e.g. trade and industry, energy, environment and transport, etc.). Thus, development cooperation revolves around twin pillars of development and pro-poor sector reform. The European Commission also indicated "thematic interventions" in the areas of democracy and human rights, migration and asylum, human and social development (capacity building for policy-makers, etc.), environment and sustainable management of natural resources including energy and non-state actors development.[25] The Union also provides humanitarian assistance in times of crisis such as floods, drought and earthquakes. This is routed through the Humanitarian Aid Office (ECHO).

Table 7.1: Overview of the Current EU Projects in India

	Sector/Category	*EU contribution (in Euros)*
1.	Conflict Prevention (Disaster prevention and preparedness in costal districts)	874,311.00
2.	Environment and the sustainable management of natural resources	2,345,031.88
3.	Governance, democracy, human rights and support for economic and institutional reforms	4,413,355.53
4.	Human Development(Empowering women, HIV prevention etc.)	20,358,683.74
5.	Infrastructure, communication and transport	4,299,300.00
6.	Multi-Sectors (Community empowerment, developing knowledgebase, health sector, revitalizing sustainable rural livelihoods etc.)	373,779,931.00
7.	Rural development, territorial planning, agriculture andfood security	2,231,680.89
8.	Trade and regional integration	1,582,301.00
9.	Water and energy	7,156,359.00
	Total	**417,040,954.04**

Source: Compilation based on EU List of Projects, at http//eeas.eu/delegations/india/projects/ list_of_projects/

The EU has also signed state partnership programmes with two states in India and has allocated about €160 million over a period of six years (2006-2012) for Chhattisgarh and Rajasthan. In Chhattisgarh, the programme seeks to increase the efficiency in the delivery of critical social services, especially health and education and the reduction of poverty of tribal communities through environment-friendly economic strategies. It has also allotted €32 million for education and €32 million for the health care system.[26] In Rajasthan, the focus is on promoting state-wide water sector reform and improvement and enhanced water supply and groundwater recharge in select areas of the state.[27]

Conclusion

The European Union is undoubtedly an important partner in development cooperation with India. The programmes envisaged are wide and deep and the goes beyond the confines of traditional development cooperation. In fact, the special report of the Court of Auditors appreciated the nature of development cooperation with India for more than two decades. It noted the efficiency of the Commission in targeting the poor by moving "above" classical rural development and infrastructure projects to the establishment of sector support programmes in health and education. The Report strongly supported structural reforms and "sustainability" results.[28] Today, areas of development cooperation today encompass exchange of views on global development issues and exploration of cooperation in development projects in third countries.

The EU is undeniably a major donor of development assistance to India. During 2007-2013, it allocated €470 million in development aid. There are concerns that development assistance may be reduced in the near future in view of the recent aid reform of October 2011, which seeks to reduce aid to 19 emerging economies, including China, India and Brazil from 2014 onwards in order to focus on the 'neediest'.[29]

An issue of concern is the increasing linkage of development assistance to EU trade policy. Indian negotiators do not contest the importance of democracy, good governance, environment protection, etc. They assert that these are domestic matters and that the requisite legal framework to safeguard them already exists. The EU has not adopted an overly normative approach in development cooperation with India and has generally tended to adopt a pragmatic approach and realist prudence.

Some civil society groups, especially those opposed to the indiscriminate globalisation and free trade agreements, however, are critical of the value-loaded words and objectives in the on-going negotiations for an India-EU bilateral trade and investment agreement. The presumption of universal applicability of the Union's preferred values and its efforts to enforce them are not looked upon favourably.[30] There are calls to respect the distinctiveness and sensitivities of the countries concerned and that the needs and capacity constraints of the countries need to be considered before integration with global market is attempted and the institutional and productive capacities need to be strengthened. Aid conditionalities result in unequal competition with more developed economies and are detrimental to large sections and also deprive governments the necessary policy space to implement their own development strategies.[31] Thus, the emphasis on structural reforms and 'smooth integration into global economy' need not necessarily lead to poverty eradication. On the contrary, it could increase the gap between the rich and the poor.

It is paradoxical that while the EU supports pro-poor policies, it also supports free trade which is unlikely to benefit all sections of people since world trade is dominated by multinational corporations. In a situation where development is skewed in favour of the rich and the powerful, the Union's universal propagation of the minimum state and multilateralism can hamper efforts to reduce poverty. Insistence on the labour clause enhances the difficulties for countries and worsens the conditions of the poor without state support. Therefore, the present development cooperation policy coupled with free trade logic, norms and political preferences is hardly effective in addressing the conditions that breed poverty and tend to lose exclusive focus on the objective of poverty eradication.

Another issue of concern is the selective interpretation of the principles of multilateralism by the EU. Despite WTO provisions, EU continues to protect sectors that are extremely important for India such as agriculture, leather and textiles by non-tariff barriers (NTBs), anti-dumping clauses, etc. The selective interpretation of multilateralism and trade liberalisation in areas beneficial to the Union (e.g. financial services and manufactured products), while ignoring other areas like agriculture, textiles, clothing and footwear and its reluctance to grant liberal access to workers ('Mode 4' services) hardly makes EU advocacy of liberalisation tenable. Other exports from India have also witnessed blatant NTBs and discriminatory trade practices as well as anti-dumping measures.[32] India has therefore been concerned about EU development cooperation linkages with trade. The imposition of conditionalities like labour clause, environmental concerns, etc. on exports by unorganised and small producers exposes them to intense global competition.

India has been critical of development assistance based on political preferences to Pakistan. New Delhi challenged the Union's decision in 2002 to extend the GSP Plus drug regime to Pakistan, which would have led to increased textile exports to the EU market in the WTO. When the dispute settlement panel gave a verdict in favour of India, Brussels incorporated such support under its broader governance framework. Indian stakeholders wondered whether acts of expediency can ever reinforce the Union's claims of being a normative power.

Despite such criticism, one cannot underestimate the advantages of EU development cooperation. India, at times, has shown weariness with the complex structure of decision-making in the EU as well as increasing political priorities in EU development cooperation. The European Union has also been mindful of Indian sensitivities. The India-EU relationship should transcend the traditional donor-recipient relationship and seek to foster flexibility and sensitivity for mutual benefit.

NOTES

1 See R. Enzo Grilli, *The European Community and Developing Countries* (Cambridge: Cambridge University Press, 1993).

2 Donor coordination of aid policies at the global level was stressed at the *Paris Declaration on Aid Effectiveness* (2005). Clause 39, for instance, states that, "Donors commit to: Harmonise their activities... It should focus on upstream analysis, joint assessments, joint strategies, co-ordination of political engagement; and practical initiatives such as the establishment of joint donor offices." See "The Paris Declaration on Aid Effectiveness and the Accra Agenda for Action," at http://www.oecd.org/dataoecd/11/41/34428351.pdf.

3 European Communities, *Treaty on European Union* (Luxembourg, 1992); Title XVIII, Article 130u. Article 130u is renumbered as Article 177 (Title XX) in the Treaty of Amsterdam.

4 Article 2 C 1, Lisbon Treaty, *Official Journal of the European Union*, 17 December 2007, at http://eur-lex.europa.eu/LexUriServ/LexUriServ.do?uri=OJ:C:2007:306:0042:0133:EN:PDF.

5 *Official Journal*, n. 3; Article 208 of the "Consolidated Version of the Treaty on the functioning of the European Union" that rearranges the Article 177 of Maastricht Treaty again stress on the poverty eradication objective.

6 See Development and Cooperation–Europeaid, http://ec.europa.eu/europeaid/how/finance/ dci_en.htm.

7 Development and Cooperation–Europeaid, http://ec.europa.eu/europeaid/how/finance/dci/ investing_en.htm.

8 http://ec.europa.eu/development/icenter/repository/F48_consultationNSAs_en_en.pdf; http://ec. europa.eu/development/icenter/repository/COMM_PDF_COM_2006_0088_F_EN_IMPACT_EUROPEEN.pdf; http://ec.europa.eu/development/icenter/repository/Framework_CSP_2006_ en.pdf.

9 http://ec.europa.eu/development/policies/consensus_en.cfm; *Official Journal of the European Union* C 46/1 24.2.2006 EN, http://ec.europa.eu/development/icenter/repository/ european_ consensus_2005_en.pdf.

10 From the mid-1990s, additional trade preferences were given or

withdrawn by the European Union to countries observing social and drug (fighting) policies. But when India challenged the addition of Pakistan by the EU in its list of the GSP drugs regime in the WTO, the EU abandoned separate social and drugs provisions and incorporated these to a broader "sustainable development and good governance" principles. Gerrit Faber and Jan Orbie, "The New Trade and Development Agenda of the European Union," *Perspectives on European Politics and Society,* 9(2), June 2008, pp. 192-207.

11 http://ec.europa.eu/development/geographical/cotonouintro_en.cfm?CFID=2311138&CFTOKEN=de5549ec566e53bc-44BE1EAC-BCAD-6AE3-85FE869240E498A7&jsessionid=243062fb88384a375d62.

12 Para 1 (a) and (b), Lisbon Treaty, n. 1.

13 http://ec.europa.eu/development/policies/9interventionareas/trade/aid-for-trade_en.cfm.

14 Commission of the European Communities, Press and Information Directorate-General, *Information Development Aid, Food Aid by the European Community, 40-73,* at http://aei.pitt.edu/12325/1/71252_1.pdf.

15 Fegerico Birocchi, "The European Union's Development Policies towards Asian and Latin American Countries," DSA *European Development Policy Study Group,* Discussion Paper No. 10, February 1999, www. Edpsg.org/Documents/DP10.doc.

16 Council Regulation (EEC) No.443/92 of 25 February 1992 on "Financial and Technical Assistance to, and Economic Cooperation with, the developing countries in Asia and Latin America," at http://europa.eu.legislation_summaries/external_relations_with_thirdcountries/latin_america/r1400/_en.htm.

17 Communication from the Commission to the Council, "Towards a New Asia Strategy," COM (94) 314 final, Brussels 13-07-1994, http://europa.eu.int/comm/external_relations/asem/asem _process/com95.htm.

18 "Global Europe Competing in the world, A contribution to the EU's Growth and Jobs Strategy," European Commission, External Trade, at http://trade.ec.europa.eu/doclib/docs/2006/october/tradoc_130376.pdf.

19 *India, Country Strategy Paper, (2007-2013),* http://eeas.europa.eu/delegations/india/documents/eu_india/country_strategy_paper_07_13_en.pdf.

20 Ibid.

21 Ibid.

22 Ibid.

23 In the earlier *Country Strategy Paper (2002-2006)*, the EU had committed an assistance of €150 million for sectoral support for primary education, €200 million for the Sarva Siksha Abhiyan and €240 million for the health sector. See http://eeas.europa.eu/india/csp /02_06_en.pdf.

24 Government of India, Ministry of Finance, *Annual Report 2010-2011*. http://finmin.nic.in/reports/AnnualReport2010-11.pdf.

25 India, *Country Strategy Paper*, n. 19.

26 http://eeas.europa.eu/delegations/india/eu_india/development_cooperation/education/index_en.htm; http://eeas.europa.eu/delegations/india/eu_india/development_cooperation/healthcare/index_ en.htm.

27 http://www.delind.ec.europa.eu/dc-sgi-nrm.asp?links=sgi-link4.

28 Special Report, No 10/2003, "concerning the effectiveness of the Commission's management of development assistance to India in targeting the poor and ensuring sustainable benefits, together with the Commission's replies", *Official Journal of the European Union*, 2003/C 211/02, http://eur-lex.europa.eu/LexUriServ/LexUriServ.do?uri=OJ:C:2003:211:0021:0037:EN:PDF.

29 "Aid Reform," at http://www.eubusiness.com/news-eu/aid-emerge.dxb/?searchterm=India; "EU launches controversial world aid reform", 13 October 2011. See http://www.eubusiness.com/news-eu/aid-economy.cwd/.

30 Dick Gupwell and Natalie Gupta, "EU FTA Negotiations with India, ASEAN and Korea: The Question of Fair Labour Standards," *Asia Europe Journal*, no. 7, 2009, p. 91; Jan Zielonka, "Europe as a Global Actor: Empire by Example?," *International Affairs,* 84(3), 2008, pp. 471-484; Lorenzo Fioramonti and Arlo Poletti, "Facing the Giant: Southern Perspectives on the European Union," *Third World Quarterly*, 29(1), 2008, pp. 167-180.

31 Marc Maes, "Civil Society Perspectives on EU-Asia Free Trade Agreements," *Asia Europe Journal*, No. 7, 2009, pp. 97-107.

32 Reviewing the NTBs levied against Indian exports by others, the Ministry of Commerce states that the Registration, Evaluation and Authorisation of Chemicals (REACH) legislation of the European Community Regulation on Chemicals and their safe use (EC 1907/2006), for instance, is likely to increase the cost of compliance by €85,000 to € 325,000 per chemical. Further, in the case of marine products, the review maintains that there is often rejection and subsequent destruction of consignments on the ground that they have

chloramphenicol/nitrofuran residues and in countries like Italy and France they are also rejected due to alleged presence of bacterial inhibitors/anti-biotic residues without any confirmatory tests. See Government of India, Department of Commerce, http://commerce.nic.in/trade/international_ntm.asp? id=4&trade=i.

8

India, the EU and Development Aid: New Context and New Realities

Sachin Chaturvedi

Introduction

The global aid architecture has undergone a major change in recent years. The Fourth High Level Forum on Aid Effectiveness (HLF-4) organized at Busan (29 November-1 December 2011) also highlighted some of the major changes in the global aid and development cooperation architecture. The current focus is how these changes can enable the global system to effectively address major impediments in moving towards the goal, which epitomized the slogan for the High Level Forum on Aid Effectiveness, viz. "Toward a Better World for All". The new architecture highlights the fact that diversity of experiences of global aid or development cooperation. The insistence of the Development Assistance Committee (DAC) of the Organization for Economic Cooperation and Development (OECD) on the Paris Declaration[1] as the only way forward faced explicit and implicit resistance not only from the non-DAC members, but also from within the DAC. At the Busan meeting, the DAC members revisited their idea of uniformity and regimented global aid governance.

The European Commission fully embraced the DAC consensus even though only 15 EU Member States are currently members of the DAC.[2] Brussels also established an EU Transparency Guarantee to increase accountability and predictability, strengthen democratic ownership and improve development results.[3] In its position paper for the Busan Summit, the Union acknowledged the emergence of South-South cooperation and triangular cooperation for development.[4]

This chapter seeks to examine whether it is possible for India and the Union to work together for evolving a shared perception on role of 'aid' and 'development partnership' for effective cooperation and if possible an enhanced triangular development cooperation. Both have sought to enhance bilateral institutional mechanisms since the early 1990s, including the Joint Commission, Sub-Commission, India-EC Macroeconomic Dialogue, etc. The focus was further expanded with the launch of the India-EU Strategic Partnership in 2004. These mechanisms have facilitated intense and detailed consultations at different levels and at regular intervals. However, despite discussions over a wide range of issues, little attention has so far been paid to developing a joint understanding of challenges confronted in enhancing global governance of aid. The European Union and India should endeavour to develop common approaches and understanding about the meaning and goals of development within a democratic framework in order to foster an effective global aid regime.

This chapter seeks to address some of these issues. It provides a brief overview of EU development assistance to India. It goes on to trace India's emergence as a major provider of development assistance. It explores the complementarities and possibilities for cooperation between India and the EU and makes some concluding observations.

EU Development Assistance to India

India has been a recipient of EU development assistance since 1976 and since then more than €2 billion have been committed.[5]

Within the European Commission, assistance to India is part of a framework known as the ALA Regulation which provides perspective on EC's engagement with Asia and Latin America. It was only in 1994 that the EC announced a new policy for Asia alone called "Towards a New Asia Strategy". This included India across various regional programmes like Asia Urbs (cooperation with local communities), Asia Link (promoting networking among universities), Asia Pro Eco (promoting environmental partnership, etc.). This strategy was upgraded in 2001 to a "Strategic Framework for Enhanced Partnership".[6] As a part of Strategic Partnership, one of the areas stressed by the Joint Action Plan (JAP) was development cooperation.[7] In this area, it was decided to focus on operationalization of State Partnership programmes with the EU assistance of €160 million and undertake an impact assessment of development schemes financed in India. The JAP also urged the two sides to explore the feasibility of launching development projects in third countries and exchange views on global development issues.[8] The EU has also chosen to focus on development cooperation for the elementary education what is officially named as *Sarva Shiksha Abhiyan* (Education for All Movement) and the National Rural Health Mission of the Government of India.

The EU is the only multilateral development assistance provider among the leading donors. (Table 8.1) In 2009-2010, India received assistance of around US $70 million, which is 1 per cent of the total incoming aid in the same year. Japan and the UK are the major bilateral donors for India with 21 per cent and 6 per cent share in total incoming aid.

A priority for EU development assistance to India has been education and health since 1991. Table 8.2 captures percentage share of budgetary allocations for the period 1991-2004 and 2005-2010, where emphasis on education is quite evident. It received almost 38 per cent of the budget in the period 1991-2004 while during 2005-2010, this went up to 48 per cent. In

Table 8.1: Major Development Assistance Providers for India, 2009-10

Country	*2009-10 (US $ Million)*
Japan	1455.3 (21%)
United Kingdom	379 (6%)
Russia Federation	204.9 (3%)
Germany	125.3 (2%)
European Economic Community	70.14 (1%)
United States	3.1 (0.05%)
Grand Total	6823.3

Source: Government of India, *Economic Survey, 2010-11,* A113-114.

case of the health sector, the budgetary allocation declined from 25 per cent to 18 per cent. In the 2005-2010 period, the allocations were made with focus on specific services and not at the broad sectoral level. For instance, in 1991-2004, allocation for agriculture was 10 per cent and that for rural development was also around 10 per cent. These heads disappeared in the following period and enhanced allocations were made for water supply and sanitation where the allocation increased from 0.7 per cent to 5.24 per cent. The period 2005-2010 also shows enhanced support for social infrastructure and services and support for civil society. Again, allocations like multi-sectoral aid, etc. have disappeared from the list. This was a marked departure from an earlier practice of supporting rural development projects. It was only after 1994, when programme-based funding became evident and in fact was stepped up following the EU-India Strategic Partnership accomplished in September 2005. This was also the year when India changed its policy for incoming aid and fixed a minimum aid at $25 million for the Indian Government to directly accept aid from any donor. At present, this is confined to the G-8 and the EU. The *Country Strategy Paper, 2007-2013* is financed under the Development Cooperation Instrument (DCI) of the European Union. The primary objective of DCI is to address poverty, sustainable development and Millennium Development Goals.

Table 8.2: Percentage share of Total Commitments by Sectors, 1991-2004 and 2005-10

Sector	*1991-2004*	*2005-10*
Education	37.69	47.69
Health	25.2	17.57
Agriculture	10.2	
Rural development	9.8	
Other emergency and distress relief	2.6	10.98
Transport and storage	2.5	1.16
Forestry	2.4	1.08
Other multisector aid	1.6	4.36
Trade	1.4	1.79
Water supply and sanitation	0.7	5.24
Government and civil society	0.7	1.32
Other social infrastructure and services	0.6	6.87
Multisector aid	0.6	
Women in development	0.4	
Banking and financial services	0.2	0.06
Energy generation and supply	0.1	0.25
Environment	0.1	0.6
Industry	0.1	0.28
Urban development and management	0.1	
Business and other services	0	0.12
Developmental food aid/food security assistance	0	
Not Specified	3	
Grand Total	**100.0**	

Source: EEC, "Evaluation of the European Commission's Support to The Republic of India, Final Report, August 2007," Evaluation for the European Commission and QWIDS, OECD.

India as a Source for Development Assistance

India has been engaged in a development partnership programme since India's independence. In 1949, India established 75 fellowships for providing training and technical assistance to partner countries. Over the years, Indian development cooperation has evolved across three major pillars, viz. capacity building and skill transfer, provision of credit lines to trade partners and assistance related to development projects. The idea of development partnership actually brings in philosophy of larger "development compact", which has elements of trade, investment and technology as its attributes.[9] This approach of engagement in development cooperation is therefore a much wider approach than the traditional one of "aid".

India is currently engaged in providing development assistance in several areas where it received aid in initial years of its development. For instance, Germany provided major support for tool rooms for the upgradation of technical skills. India is now providing assistance in this very area. Norway had provided assistance in the health sector, including the establishment of the All India Institute of Medical Sciences in New Delhi. India is currently supporting health infrastructure across the African continent by opening primary health centres and providing expert knowledge through a tele-medicine e-network established as a Pan African network.

Bhutan, Nepal, Sri Lanka and Bangladesh have occupied a key position in India's development assistance till the early 2000s. India provided both programme and project-based assistance to several of its neighbours. In the case of Nepal and Bhutan, a major component of Indian support has been through the financing of Five Year Plans. Since 2003, India made a conscious decision of diversifying to other geographical areas, especially Southeast Asia, Latin America and Africa.

In Southeast Asia, India has responded to the appeal of the ASEAN Secretariat to bridge the development gap among ASEAN members. The joint declaration on "ASEAN-India Partnership for Peace, Progress and Shared Prosperity" adopted at the third ASEAN-India Summit (Vientiane, 30 November 2004) referred to the formation of a more integrated ASEAN Community comprising the ASEAN Security Community, the ASEAN Economic Community and the ASEAN Socio-

Cultural Community. India pledged support for the idea of an ASEAN Economic Community. New Delhi decided to provide support for entrepreneurship development to Cambodia, Laos, Myanmar and Vietnam (CLMV) leading to the establishment of four National Institutes for Entrepreneurship Development in these countries.

India adopted a strategy of establishing similar institutions in Africa where it has drawn up long-term engagement plans for the region and has identified various areas for capacity creation (Table 8.3). In keeping with the decision taken at the first India-Africa Forum Summit (2008), the Indian Government resolved to establish 21 institutions in Africa. The major ones include all the key areas of economic activity,

Table 8.3: Indian Institutional Support in Africa

Country	*Amount*	*Objectives*
Ethiopia	$ 640 million	Improving sugar production facilities
Botswana	—	Agriculture research, farm machinery production.
Ghana	$27 million	Finance projects with poverty alleviation
	$2 million	India-Ghana Kofi Annan Centre of Excellence in Information and communication technology
Tanzania	$4 million	Small scale industry development
NEPAD	$200 million	Pan-African Satellite/Fiber Optic Network
Senegal	$15 million concessional line of credit.	Production of agricultural equipments
Zimbabwe	$2.8 million	Indo-Zimbabwe Technology Centre at the Harare Institute of Technology and at Bulawayo Polytechnic
Benin	US$ 10 million	Telecommunication Consultants India Limited (TCIL) has executed projects to provide telecom network in Porto Novo and twin-cities of Abomey and Bohicon.

Source: Compiled by the author.

including the India-Africa Institute of Foreign Trade at Kampala, Uganda; the India-Africa Diamond Institute at Gaborone, Botswana; the India-Africa Institute of Educational Planning and Administration at Bujumbura, Burundi; and the India-Africa Institute of Information Technology in Ghana.

India has launched several initiatives to engage in areas of economic and commercial importance for partner countries so as to catalyze their growth prospects through a vibrant partnership. In case of Africa, the New Delhi Africa Summit (2008) identified science and technology, R&D cooperation, tourism, pro-poor growth strategies, infrastructure, energy and environment and communication infrastructure as key areas for bilateral engagement.

Half of the Exim Bank's operative lines of credit as on 7 February 2012 were for Africa with 39 per cent for South Asia. The rest of the credits were focused on Central Asia (6 per cent), Asia (3 per cent) and Latin America (2 per cent).[10]

Global Aid Architecture and EU-India Partnership

The Busan Outcome Document calls for a constructive dialogue between donors and development recipients for "effective" global governance of aid. It acknowledges the fact that in times of recession and contracting economies we must pool resources for optimal returns and better outcomes. However, one must acknowledge that the High Level Forum on Aid Effectiveness is a DAC platform for interaction between donors and recipients. Over the years, however, it has also taken a keen interest in the providers of South-South Cooperation. After the Third High-Level Forum, popularly called as Accra Summit in September 2008, a special Task Team on South-South Cooperation, facilitated by various international agencies, was launched for collecting evidence from all over the world, in the form of case studies on South-South cooperation. It is in this backdrop that the idea of common but differentiated responsibilities is being discussed in various fora, where future directions for aid and development cooperation are being examined. The idea of common but differentiated responsibilities can work best when there is an appreciation to learn from various processes involving development partnerships across the globe and understand alternate views on development cooperation and its ramifications. In this context, if emerging economies are being considered to be a part of the solution, then they must also be given space to make their contributions in global policy-setting processes at neutral policy platforms.

The net ODA from the DAC in 2010 was nearly US$129 billion and constituted 0.32 per cent of DAC Gross National Income (GNI). Of this amount, nearly US$29.3 billion was for Africa, including US$27 billion for Sub-Saharan Africa. Among DAC donors, the share of 15 DAC EU members was nearly US$70 billion. The largest donors were the USA (US$29 billion), France (US$13 billion), Germany (US$12 billion) and Japan (US$11 billion). (Table 8.4)

Table 8.4: Main DAC Donors and their Aid Quantum

Country	*Quantum of ODA (current US$ billion)*	*ODA share in GNI (per cent)*	*Share in DAC Flows*
USA	29	0.21	22.5
France	13	0.47	10.1
Germany	12	0.35	9.3
Japan	11	0.18	8.5
Sub Total	**65**		**50.4**
Total DAC	**129**		**100.0**

Source: OECD DAC 2011.

The Declaration on Harmonization, adopted at the High-level Forum of donor agencies in Rome in February 2003, led to the creation of the DAC Working Party on Aid Effectiveness and Donor Practices (WP-EFF).[11] Since its establishment, the WP-EFF has been the principal forum for discussion on issues of aid effectiveness and development priorities in the context of official development assistance. The Second High Level Forum (Paris, 2005) led to the adoption of the Paris Declaration with five major principles, viz. ownership, alignment, harmonisation, managing the results and last, but not the least, mutual accountability. It was only at the Third High Level Forum (Accra, September 2008) that a detailed working agenda was adopted.

In recent years, we have witnessed an intense debate on similarities and differences between North-South and South-South cooperation. Some national governments and the DAC launched the Task Team on South–South Cooperation (TT-SSC) for collecting evidence from various case studies on South-South cooperation in order to explore possible areas of convergence between the two modalities of engagement, viz. South-South cooperation and North-South cooperation from the point of view of the Paris Declaration. A report from the TT-SSC presented 154 case studies and more are in the pipeline. It is high time that one focused on the perspectives of recipients and move beyond the notion of "donors" and "partners". It may not be in collective interest to reject ideas of "development partnership" espoused by the South or aid-related principles coming from DAC.

There is ample scope for coexistence of both the modalities and opportunities for mutual learning. Diversity is what comes from our experiences and we should learn to cherish this. We must now confront serious questions like "How effective is aid to have "development impact with these countries?" and "Would triangular cooperation accelerate the process?"

It is time is to focus on components of aid programmes and move away from the rigidities of framework-based approaches which only results in delays in both approvals and implementation. The DAC must show flexibility and embrace new approaches. We must seek to evolve the concept of "development effectiveness" and introduce the idea of participation with the private sector and civil society organisations as points of convergence for both the North and the South.

Development Compact

In an increasingly interdependent world, there is a need for responses that are truly global. To that end, we need to evolve frameworks that introduce the best options available from our experiences of recent years. The Seoul G-20 Summit (2010) agreed on a series of policy actions designed to respond to the development-related challenges being faced by the global community. This was a follow-up on the mandate for establishing a Working Group on Development reached at the 2009 G-20 Summit at Toronto. The group was chaired by South Korea along with South Africa at the Seoul G-20 Summit (11-12 November 2012), at the initiative of South Korea, "development" was included as a substantive item on the G-20 agenda for the first time in its history.

The Seoul Consensus advocated "growth with resilience". To that end, it emphasized the declining dependence on aid and the promotion of social protection schemes through mobilization of domestic resources. It also suggested better market access possibilities for the Least Developed Countries (LDCs) by provision of duty-free, quota-free access and by the promotion of regional trade agreements in Africa. It also identified necessity of providing access to capital markets for small and medium enterprises, the virtues of investment promotion and the need for both knowledge building and knowledge transfer. Thus, the Seoul Consensus sets the stage for policy-makers to move in the direction of broadening aid policies to encompass development cooperation. Development cooperation should henceforth include commitments to work in partnership with developing countries with a multi-year action plan on development.

The focus of emerging economies on productive sectors, which directly contribute in the economic development, signifies what is increasingly being termed as "development compact". There is need to promote investment mechanisms for fostering the growth of productive engagements, including innovative sources of funding. For instance, some of them like the Global Action Initiative against Hunger and Poverty, the Leading Group on Solidarity Levies to Fund Development, and the India–Brazil–South Africa (IBSA) Fund may also help in meeting social challenges. Several leading developing countries have come forward to help other developing countries through supporting international mechanisms. For example, South Africa committed US$20 million for the next 20 years at the GAVI Alliance (Global Alliance for Vaccines and Immunization). Brazil, China, India and South Africa have committed more than US$40 million in total to support various activities of the Global Fund to Fight AIDS, Tuberculosis and Malaria (GFATM). Apart from providing major cash support to various international initiatives, such as the Global Fund for addressing Tropical Diseases, these countries also support enhancement of capacity to produce drugs, vaccines and diagnostic kits in various developing countries. A number of developing countries are also participating in debt relief initiatives on both a bilateral and a multilateral basis. This approach needs to be strengthened across the board through the development of social sector. EU Member States have special expertise in supporting diverse social sectors to foster balanced societal development. Efforts to promote synergy would ensure sustainable and balanced development in the recipient economies. Enhancement of the role of partner countries in leading aid delivery cooperation is a key for success of aid delivery and eventually contributing to the growth process. This would also help in moving in the direction of going beyond aid for LDCs.

Conclusion

The European Union has accepted all the five principles adopted under the Paris Declaration, viz. ownership, alignment, harmonization, managing the results, and mutual accountability. As a result, the Union is committed to aid processes and on improvement of aid delivery and utilization, including the basic goals of greater efficiency and effectiveness. There is increasing emphasis on donor harmonization, national ownership of development plans, and sound policies on the part of the recipients. However, the work agenda on the rest of the principles and their role continues as well. The Report on the Implementation of the Paris Declaration concluded that the Development Assistance Committee is still far from achieving quantum targets for aid and that the DAC member States are still very far from ensuring the "quality" of aid as originally perceived by the DAC.[12]

The Busan Outcome Document provides a roadmap for greater engagement of both DAC and non-DAC members since it categorically acknowledges North-South cooperation as well as South-South Cooperation when it states that "the nature, modalities and responsibilities that apply to South-South cooperation differ from those that apply to North-South cooperation". It is important that the distinction between North-South aid and South-South cooperation is elaborated in order to avoid any confusion on the respective obligations of the developed and the developing countries at a time when there are prospects of the reform of the global aid architecture are mentioned in the Busan Outcome Document.

There is a greater degree of transparency and accountability since India reports all dimensions of its development strategy and related budgetary allocations to the Indian Parliament. Indian programmes, projects and other initiatives are in any case bound by the idea of mutual accountability since almost all these initiatives are based on specific requests from partner countries.

At present, India is mostly engaged on its own in most of the member countries, except where specific requests from third countries are accepted. As a result, there is a limited level of engagement with triangular cooperation. Collaboration between the European Union and India may facilitate the evolution of a "balanced" aid strategy for addressing wider global challenges. This may be tried at the interim group which has come up at the Ad hoc Working Party on Aid Effectiveness. India may also independently explore working with EU on project peer review processes, which is an established practice across all DAC members for improvisations on Indian aid practices.

NOTES

1 The Paris Declaration on Aid Effectiveness was adopted in 2005 at the Second High Level Forum on Aid Effectiveness hosted by OECD-DAC, with five principles, viz. ownership, alignment, harmonization, managing the results and last, but not the least, mutual accountability.

2 Sven Grimm, John Humphrey, Erik Lundsgaarde and Sarah-Lea John de Sousa, "European Development Cooperation to 2020: Challenges by New Actors in International Development," *Working Paper No. 4*, 2009.

3 European Commisison, Press Release, "The European Union announces new initiatives to increase transparency and improve coordination in aid delivery," IP/11/1472, 30 November 2011, at http://europa.eu/rapid/press-release_IP-11-1472_en.htm?locale=en.

4 Proposal for the EU Common Position for the 4th High Level Forum on Aid Effectiveness, Busan. Commission Communication, Brussels, 7.9.2011 COM(2011) 541 final. (Doc. 13927/11).

5 European Commission, "Evaluation of the European Commission's Support to The Republic of India, Final Report, August 2007."

6 Ibid.

7 The other areas being industrial policy, science and technology, finance and monetary affairs, environment, energy, information and communication technologies, transport, shipping, space technology, pharmaceuticals and biotechnology, agriculture, customs, employment and social policy, business cooperation and development cooperation.

8 European Union, "Global Partners for Global Challenges: The EU-

India Joint Action Plan (JAP)," EU-India Summit, Marseilles, 29 September 2008.

9 Sachin Chaturvedi, "Beyond the Slogan of South-South Co-operation: Exploring 'Development Compact' and New Dynamics of South-South Cooperation," Paper presented at the Barnes Symposium entitled "Legitimacy, Economic Development and Change Revisited" at the USC Law School, University of Carolina, Columbia, 13-14 April 2012.

10 Export-Import Bank of India, "Online Exim Bank's Operative Lines of Credit," updated as on 7 February 2012.

11 OECD, "Rome Declaration on Harmonisation', Harmonising Donor Practices For Effective Aid Delivery" (Paris: OECD, 2003).

12 Danish Institute for International Studies, "The Evaluation of the Paris Declaration – Phase 2, May 2011".

9

China, India and the Eurozone Crisis

Rajendra K. Jain

Introduction

The Eurozone crisis is probably the most severe crisis that the European Union has faced in its history. It is testing the EU to its limits – economically, politically, socially, and democratically – and has far reaching global consequences. It is an economic crisis that became a political crisis because of a number of inherent flaws – the absence of a fiscal union to sustain it, weak diligence in strictly enforcing the convergence criteria of the monetary union in the wake of violations Member States, the lack of a common treasury, or for an exit mechanism from Euroland. The Eurozone crisis is closely related to loss of competitiveness which has landed many European countries in the current financial mess. It is also a political crisis with European politicians confronting difficult choices, with many governments having been toppled as a result of the austerity drive. Politicians know exactly what to do, but the problem is that they also know that if they do the right thing, they will not be re-elected.

The Eurozone sovereign debt crisis has led to the proliferation of news items in the Asian media and put the Union under greater scrutiny by Asian elites and media as the EU became "even more 'inward looking' due to its financial and economic woes, but the image of the 'sick man Europe' trapped in a severe crisis has captivated the attention of international media, general publics and stakeholders.[1] While the media tends "to pursue sensationalized news exaggerating negativity and conflict, the general public and elites displayed positive and constructive visions of the EU despite times of crisis."[2]

China and the Eurozone Crisis

China has a strong interest in continued economic growth because the EU is its largest trading partner accounting for €429 billion two-way trade in goods in 2011 with a €156 billion trade surplus. The Eurozone sovereign debt crisis, according Chinese policy-makers and academics, has been triggered by government failure, over-borrowed debts, the banking crisis, and systemic flaws and deficiencies in the Eurozone. European leaders, they argue, display a lack of political will and seek to avoid making difficult choices. Some progress, they felt, had been made in the Eurozone in terms of responding to debt troubles, especially by adopting austerity measures and injecting liquidity in the market, but these steps were not considered adequate to solve the fundamental problem.[3] The admission of countries with different socio-economic structures and less developed welfare systems, some Chinese observers felt, has signified that due to limited country-to-country transfers, the new entrants sought to acquire more debt in an attempt to catch up with their richer Western counterparts.[4]

European countries perceived China as a potential Santa Claus which would use its foreign exchange reserves of over $3.3 trillion to come to the rescue of the European economies in distress. In October 2010, Premier Wen Jiabao said China would buy Greek bonds to support Greece's shipping industry while Chinese state-run banks agreed to $268 million in loans to three Greek shippers. In April 2011, Spanish Prime Minister secured a Chinese pledge to invest in his nation's faltering savings bank and in government debt. In June 2011, Premier Wen Jiabao offered a helping hand to Europe by buying a limited volume of sovereign bonds. China pledged to buy Hungarian government bonds and agreed a Euro 1 billion loan for the financing of development projects in the country.

The Chinese have preferred to go through the International Monetary Fund (IMF) to provide funds for heavily indebted countries in order to probably set a precedent as to how it would act in future international bailouts. At the G-20 summit in June 2012, China announced that it would contribute $43 billion to a new IMF instrument that could be used to help distressed Eurozone countries.

Europeans have tended to overestimate and overstate Chinese capabilities to assist the Eurozone. China, in fact, does not have adequate resources to finance the enormous requirements of Europe. The Chinese have also become more risk averse after the 2008 financial crisis. Given the opacity and lack of transparency about Chinese purchases of Eurobonds since China does not publish the breakdown by country, one does not really know what the actual Chinese holdings of European debt are. Experts estimate Chinese purchases of Eurozone bonds from crisis-ridden countries like Greece and Portugal remain in the lower single-digit billion range. The bulk of China's foreign currency reserves are reported to be held in long-term sovereign instruments leaving it with only a small fraction in highly liquid short-term paper. China is estimated to have purchased about 30 per cent of the bonds issued by the European Financial Stability Facility established to bail-out the Eurozone economies. It is also estimated that a quarter of its $3.3 trillion foreign currency reserves are held in Euros.

Strong political statements by China of support to Eurozone member countries have served to temporarily reassure markets, get political goodwill and to be seen as helping interdependence and stabilizing the global economy. It is useful for China's public diplomacy to suggest that it is "a potential benefactor".[5] China has not proved to be the white knight coming to rescue Europe in distress. Until now "no grand deals have been struck in Chinese involvement has been that of a normal market actor rather than a saviour of the Eurozone."[6]

Chinese public opinion has been hostile to bailing out "the decadent" Europeans who are seen to have lived beyond their means. Aiding Europe creates the impression that China is bailing out rich foreigners with a per capita income which is four times their won at the expense of its own citizens. The Chinese have stressed the need for European to "work a bit harder... work a bit longer" like Chinese citizens and have been critical of "sloth-inducing" labour laws in Europe. There are growing concerns in China about the social and political fallout of austerity measures which had stretched the public's tolerance "to breaking point".[7]

Until recently, Chinese policy-makers and financial elites considered European integration to be an irreversible one-way process. For Chinese elites, the widespread assumption that Europe would mean a rising standard of living and social security for all Europeans has been badly dented by accumulated debt, declining global competitiveness and the crisis of the Eurozone. With almost all political energy and resources concentrated in trying to resolve the Eurozone crisis, Asian political elites were skeptical about the EU's present and potential role in international politics.

For Chinese companies, the Eurozone crisis represents an opportunity to enhance their investments in Europe, gain access to technology, increase market access, and acquire distribution networks. Chinese investment in the EU has been concentrated in a small number of countries (France, Germany and the United Kingdom). Major Chinese investments include €500 million ($645 million) by the Chinese state-owned company Cosco, which acquired the rights to container port of Piraeus for 35 years, with an additional five years. What has surprised Europeans is the doubling of cargo traffic in the first year of acquisition. In 2012, Chinese investment in Europe reached a record level of $10 billion. These included the purchase of a £600 million stake in Thames Water in January and a £450 million stake in Heathrow Airport in November.

The Europeans have also been concerned about investments by Chinese sovereign wealth funds which was initially perceived as a major threat to European economies with most European governments establishing a rhetorical link between transparency of the investor and the openness of the European market. But the deepening economic crisis shifted Europe's perception of China from foe to friend again. European heads of state and government showed "a high degree of pragmatism bordering on opportunistic behavior when they discovered the same countries whose funds they wanted to put under control as potential saviours of the world financial system."[8] Notwithstanding concerns over transparency, the prospect of increasing inward direct investment by Chinese sovereign wealth funds has been generally welcomed by the cash-strapped states of the EU.

In its efforts to win friends and influence the new Member States, Prime Minister Wen Jiabao held the first-ever summit in Poland with ten Central European Member States of the EU and six Balkan states in April 2012. The Chinese Premier met all the leaders in bilateral meetings and offered €10 billion of cheap credits for infrastructure projects. The summit is likely to become an annual event and Beijing has established a secretariat under Vice Foreign Minister Song Tao within its Foreign Ministry to coordinate relations with this group. China is seeking to build a coalition of friends in both West and East Europe, which can provide Beijing with increased leverage in times of need.[9] In the summit, more than 750 companies including 300 Chinese firms took part. Before the summit, China had invested €620 million in Central and Eastern Europe.[10] German companies have been annoyed by rapid Chinese inroads into their backyard and accused Chinese companies of resorting to price dumping aggressive financing and generous risk guarantees from Beijing as methods used by state Chinese companies to undermine their European rivals in the region.[11]

India and the Eurozone Crisis

The sovereign debt crisis, which started in the peripheral economies of the Eurozone, was peveived in India as a result of issues relating to medium-term fiscal consolidation, the exposure of European banks to public and private debt, and recurring differences in the ways to resolve the crisis had dampened global growth since the Eurozone accounted for about one fifth of global GDP.[12] Leading EU Member States, especially Germany and France, were perceived as resorting to various 'Band-Aid solutions'[13] in dealing with the crises such as bailout packages for Ireland, Greece and Portugal and keeping things on hold for the next few years. The repeated attempts to sort out the problems of the Eurozone in high profile summits has not resulted in any lasting solution but only raised expectations and made things worse.[14] There was concern about the persistently high rates of unemployment and the social fallout in the peripheral economies, which had sharply polarized the public debate on the appropriate economic policies to be adopted.[15] Admitting that some measure of austerity was necessary because government debts had blown out of proportion, Chief Economic Adviser Raghuram Rajan remarked, but "you don't want to have that level of austerity that you get riots on the streets and that the economy itself gets paralysed".[16]

The global slowdown due to the unfolding of the Eurozone sovereign debt crisis has, *inter alia*, impacted the Indian economy through the deceleration in exports, the widening of the trade and current account deficit, the decline in capital flows, the fall in the value of the Indian Rupee, the stock market decline and lower economic growth.[17] Owing to the significant integration of the Indian economy with the Eurozone, which accounted for about 19 per cent of global GDP, most of the impact of the sovereign debt crisis has been through trade and financial channels.

Despite the diversification of both destinations and products in recent years, Indian exports were adversely affected by the Eurozone crisis. The share of India's exports to Eurozone to total exports had come down from 20.1 per cent in 2009-2010 to 18.6 per cent in 2010-2011 and 17.5 per cent in 2011-2012.[18] India-EU trade declined from €80.2 billion in 2011 to €75.8 billion in 2012. Indian exports to the EU declined by around 5 per cent from €39.3 billion in 2011 to €37.3 billion in 2012. Indian imports from the EU also declined from € 40.4 billion in 2011 to €38.5 billion in 2012.[19]

Volatility in capital flows resulting from the spillover effects of monetary policy choices and other uncertainties in the advanced financial markets further impacted exchange rates and made the task of macroeconomic management difficult in many emerging economies.[20] It has led to a sharp decline in inflows of Foreign Institutional Investors (FIIs), which, in turn, led to a sharp fall in Indian stock markets.

India has been concerned that banks in the Eurozone could deleverage by reducing their lending to emerging market economies. The recapitalization needs of various Eurozone banking systems may also have an impact on credit ûows to economies of emerging powers. As the Eurozone crisis intensified, cross-border bank lending to emerging markets has dropped sharply since the second half of 2011. The Eurozone crisis was likely to have a limited impact on Indian banks since they had no presence in Portugal, Italy, Greece and Spain. None of the Indian banks had any exposure to bonds issued by Portugal, Greece and Spain, while their exposure to Italian bonds was insignificant. The funding dependence of overseas branches of Indian banks on European entities, except for the UK, was also not very significant.[21] The consolidated claims of the European banks in India, according to the Executive Director of the Reserve Bank of India, declined from US$146 billion in December 2010 to US$139 billion in December 2012. If British and Swiss banks were excluded, the European banks' claim on India stood at US$56 billion at end-December 2012.[22] While the share of borrowings from Eurozone in total foreign bank borrowings was to the extent of 17.9 per cent, borrowings from Eurozone banks as share of domestic credit was at 4.4 per cent. Indian banking system has not been notably impacted by the Euro debt crisis as neither does it have any significant presence in countries impacted by the current crisis nor Indian banks have any significant exposures to bonds issued by them.[23]

The EU is also one of the largest sources of Foreign Direct Investment for India. FDI inflows from the EU into India increased from €3.5 billion in 2009 to €7.5 billion in 2010 and €14.19 billion in 2011. Indian investment into the EU saw a decline from €0.945 billion in 2009 to €0.48 billion in 2010 but rose again in 2011 to nearly €2 billion. The leading EU Member State investors in India in 2011 were the UK (€8.24bn), Germany (€2.66 billion), Italy (€0.7 billlion), France (€0.6 billion) and Sweden (€0.55 billion), followed by Spain, Finland and Netherlands with €0.22 billion, €0.19 and €0.18 billion respectively.[24]

Travel receipts have also suffered because of lower tourist arrivals in India since Europe accounts for about one third of total tourist arrivals in India.

A survey (August 2011) conducted by the Federation of Indian Chambers of Commerce and Industry (FICCI) of Indian companies doing business and/or investments in Europe concluded that the economic turmoil had led to a loss in terms of business generation, and nearly a third of the companies had begun to look beyond Europe and geographically diversify in Africa, the Middle East, and South Asia. Over a quarter of the companies pointed out that instead of facilitating foreign investments and business, European governments were imposing a lot of policy and regulatory impediments to business practices.[25] However, many Indian companies were still on the lookout to enhance their investments in the EU since the fundamental reasons to invest in the EU had not changed. To maximise their benefits and to alleviate their business losses in terms of the reduced demands in European markets, Indian manufacturers were aggressively pursuing new business plans (including increased imports of high-end machinery and technology from Europe due to the highly competitive prices being offered by European exporters).[26]

Conclusion

China continues to regard the economic fundamentals in Europe to be still strong and European economies can recover and grow provided they undertake structural reform and exercise budgetary controls. Instead of making major diversification in its currency reserves into European bonds, China made "a sober but not exactly a game-changing contribution" to solving the Eurozone crisis.[27]

India regards the Eurozone crisis to be a deeper crisis than the 2008 global financial meltdown. Proposals regarding the formation of an Asian Monetary Union and a single regional currency have not reached made much progress so far. Full-fledged integration in the region will require creation of a supranational institution on the lines of EU but that is just a far-fetched thing at this juncture. The lessons from the not so happy experience of European integration through a monetary union mechanism will also weigh on the minds of the Asian policy-makers. In any case, the greater integration and internationalisation of Asian currencies would require an agreement between the participating countries to be bound by collective decisions rather than bilateral ones.[28]

As a result of the impact of the global financial crisis and the follow-on Eurozone crisis, central banking around the world is changing in dramatic ways. It has led to vigorous debates in India and elsewhere about autonomy and accountability of central banks, what mandate they must pursue with regard to monetary policy. The Eurozone crisis, the Reserve Bank of India acknowledged, would lead to changes in central banking everywhere, including India but it is still not clear what these changes would be.[29] Amongst the lessons that India learnt from the Eurozone crisis were that financial markets were not "self-correcting" and that "price stability and macroeconomic stability do not guarantee financial stability. We also learnt that no country is an island. Although the crisis originated in advanced economies, emerging economies too were affected, indeed by much more than they had thought possible. The contagion brought home a simple message. In a rapidly globalizing world, national and international financial stability are interlinked. They are really two sides of the same coin."[30] Other lessons that India learnt from the Eurozone crisis were financial markets were not "self-correcting" and that a collection of rational financial institutions does not necessarily make a rational financial sector.[31]

NOTES

1 These are findings of a research project assessing EU perceptions in ten Asia Europe Meeting (ASEM) "Asian" member states. Natalia Chaban and Martin Holland, "Europe in Times of Crisis: Perceptions from the Asia-Pacific," *ZEI Regional Integration Observer*, 6(2), August 2012, p. 7.

2 Ibid., p. 8.

3 "Euro debt crisis affecting Asia," *China Daily*, 3 April 2012.

4 Shi Zhiqin, "Understanding China-EU Relations," 15 October 2012, at http://carnegietsinghua.org/2012/10/15/understanding-china-eu-relations/exk6.

5 Francois Godemont and Jonas Parello-Plesner, *The Scramble for Europe*, European Council on Foreign Relations, Policy Brief ECFR/37, July 2011, p. 4.

6 Andrew Small, "China, the Eurozone Crisis and Transatlantic Relations," Testimony to the US-China Economic and Security Review

Commission, 19 April 2012, at origin.ww.uscc.gov/sites/default/files/4.19.12small.pdf.

7 Remarks by Jin Liqun, Chair of the Supervisory Board of the $480 billion China Investment Corporation. Cited in Tania Branigan, "China Sovereign Wealth Fund Official warns on Eurozone Security," *The Telegraph*, 16 November 2012.

8 Joern-CarstenGottwald, "Europe and China: Convergence, Politicization and Assertiveness," *East Asia*, 2, 2010, pp. 89-92.

9 Zhiqin, n. 4.

10 "China-Central Europe Trade and Industry summit in Warsaw," New Europe Online, 26 April 2013, at http://www.neurope.eu/article/china-central-europe-trade-and-industry-summit-warsaw

11 Antoaneta Becker, "China Expands Reach in East Europe," *Asia Times*, 2 November 2010, at http://www.atimes.com/atimes/China_Business/LK02Cb01.html.

12 India, Ministry of Finance, "India and the Global Economy," *Economic Survey, 2010-2011*, p. 338.

13 Shyam Saran, "The Coming Global Crisis – Is India Ready?", *Business Standard*, 21 September 2011.

14 Economic Advisory Council to the Prime Minister, *Review of the Economy 2011/12*, February 2012, p. 2, at pmindia.nic.in/getdoc.php?id=7AH9YZ287.pdf.

15 India, Ministry of Finance, "India and the Global Economy," *Economic Survey, 2010-2011*, pp. 338-339.

16 "India must not take Eurozone Crisis Lightly: Chief Economic Advisor Raghuram Rajan," *Economic Times*, 23 August 2012.

17 Written Reply by Finance Minister Pranab Mukherjee to the Rajya Sabha, 21 May 2012. "Eurozone crisis behind rupee fall, RBI may intervene: FM," 22 May 2012, at http://www.moneycontrol.com/news/rupee/eurozone-crisis-behind-rupee-fall-rbi-may-intervene-fm_707876.html; "Eurozone Crisis behind Falling Rupee: PM," *The Times of India*, 30 May 2012.

18 Reserve Bank of India, *Monthly Bulletin*, 66(6), June 2012, p. 1121.

19 http://www.indembassy.be/pages.php?id=53#sthash. aqse0GQN.dpuf.

20 Ministry of Finance, "India and the Global Economy," *Economic Survey, 2010-2011*, p. 338.

21 Written reply by Minister of State for Finance Namo Narain Meena to the Lok Sabha, 30 August 2012. Cited in *The Tribune* (Chandigrah), 31 August 2012.

22 Deepak Mohanty, "Impact of Euro Area Crisis on South Asia," Paper presented at the SAARCFINANCE Group Meeting, Islamabad, 18 June 2013. (http://www.rbi.org.in/scripts/BS_Speeches View.aspx?Id=815).

23 Vighneswara Swamy, "Euro Zone Debt Crisis: Implications for Indian Banking Sector," IBS – Hyderabad, 15. June 2013 Online at http://mpra.ub.uni-muenchen.de/47658/MPRA Paper No. 47658.

24 http://www.indembassy.be/pages.php?id=53#sthash. aqse0GQN.dpuf.

25 Federation of Indian Chambers of Commerce and Industry, *Current Economic Scenario in Europe and Its Impact on Indian Industry, A FICCI Survey, August 2011*. Online: http://ficci.com/SEDocument/20150/ficci-Survey-Report-Europe.pdf.

26 Ibid.

27 European Council on Foreign Relations, *European Foreign Policy Scorecard 2013* (London), January 2013, p. 26.

28 G. Padmanabhan, "Internationalisation and Integration of Asian Capital Markets: Expanded Role for Asian Currencies including the Renminbi," Comments submitted by G. Padmanabhan, Executive Director, Reserve Bank of India circulated at the OMFIF-LKY Asia's Role in the Global Economy Forum, Singapore, 12 July 2013, *RBI Monthly Report*, p. 125.

29 Reserve Bank of India, *Monthly Bulletin,* 68(3), August 2013, pp. 65-66.

30 "Central Banking in Emerging Economies: Emerging Challenges," speech delivered by Duvvuri Subbarao, Governor of the Reserve Bank of India at the European Economics and Financial Centre, London, 17 July 2013. Reserve Bank of India, *Monthly Bulletin,* 68(3), August 2013, pp. 77-78.

31 Ibid., p. 78.

10

India and the Eurozone Sovereign Debt Crisis

Karina Jędrzejowska

Introduction

When the subprime crisis spread across the globe in 2008, its impact was first noticeable in the high-income developed economies. Even though some contagion was observed in the developing world, rates of growth of most emerging economies remained relatively stable, contributing to their growing integration with global markets. Shortly after the global economy has shown signs of recovery, some European countries entered a new phase of financial difficulties. Economic slowdown and increased government spending during the subprime crisis haveresulted in growing fiscal deficits and higher levels of public debt in many European Union (EU) Member States. By the end of 2009, the Greek and Irish public debt reached an unsustainable level leading to credit downgrades and increased debt-servicing costs. As symptoms of the European sovereign debt crisis spread to more EU countries, questions were increasingly raised as to its likely impact on the Euro and emerging markets. The Union is expected to grow by only 0.6 per cent in 2012, and growth prospects for other developed economies, including the United States, are not much brighter.[1]

The EU's financial health is of key concern for emerging markets like India, whose economy has become more integrated with global markets. In recent years, the contagion from the subprime crisis has proved to be more severe for the Indian economy than initial forecasts, and growth prospects for India are not as favourable as they seemed a decade ago. In November 2011, Finance Minister Pranab Mukherjee remarked that the financial crisis in Europe was likely to adversely affect Indian growth. These concerns seem to be justified since the EU is India's largest trading partner and the Euro is a reserve currency second only to the US Dollar.[2]

This chapter seeks to analyse the impact of the debt crisis in the developed world on India. Given India's growing linkages with the global economy, the financial crisis in Europe is likely to adversely affect the Indian economy, and India's GDP growth rate may slow down. The first section of the chapter discusses the key characteristics of the sovereign debt crisis in the Eurozone and examines the possible impact of developments within the Eurozone on Asian emerging markets. The chapter then goes on to briefly analyse the current condition of the Indian economy and the impact on Indian trade and financial markets. The last section presents concluding remarks.

Sovereign Debt Crisis in the Eurozone

Questions related to sovereign debt, the debt crisis and sovereign defaults have tended to be at the forefront of international policy debate. In recent decades, there have been a series of debt crises in developing countries has taken place and additional cases of default are likely to follow. Recent developments within the Euro area indicate that high-income countries are also vulnerable to debt-servicing difficulties.[3]

Though first recorded defaults date back to antiquity, debt crises became a common phenomenon in the nineteenth and twentieth centuries. The 1980s were especially supposed to be the time of "the" debt crisis when many developing countries encountered severe debt-servicing difficulties leading to their exclusion from international capital markets and economic recession. By the early 1990s, the debt problem seemed to be under control: growth was reviving and major debtors had reached "Brady Plan" agreements to reduce bank debts. However, since the tequila crisis in Mexico in 1994, the frequency of sovereign defaults has increased. In 1997, the Asian crisis, while not initially a sovereign debt problem, turned into one as public sectors guaranteed private sector external debts, and shortly afterwards Russia defaulted on large parts of its domestic and foreign debt. More recently, in 2001, drastic devaluation and ensuing debt default in Argentina marked the largest sovereign default in the history.[4]

In the last three decades, sovereign debt crises have been confined to developing countries. In the aftermath of the global subprime crisis, the likelihood of sovereign default became very likely for even the world's most advanced economies. Since 2009 debt problems of some European countries have become one of the major problems for global markets. Economic activities of five European nations – often described as the PIIGS (Portugal, Ireland, Italy, Greece and Spain) – have come under increased scrutiny from the international community due to their rapid indebtedness and possible default. Subsequently, the magnitude of the European debts became evident. It was discovered that their indebtedness was far greater than that of Argentina in the early 2000s. The Greek debt is more than five times bigger: almost US$500 billion against less than a US$100 billion. The Italian debt, the second biggest debt-to-GDP ratio after Greece, is even larger – about US$2.5 trillion. According to EU regulations, it is impossible to bail-out an insolvent state.[5] Sovereign default within the European Union should be avoided by keeping the ceilings of fiscal deficit and public debt. These regulations, however, proved insufficient and ineffective. The current problems confirmed what manyeconomists have been long aware of. The Eurozone does not fulfil all the optimum currency area requirements. Moreover, a monetary union cannot remain effective without a support in form of a fiscal union.[6]

European sovereign debt crisis is believed to have started with the growing Greek fiscal deficit and debt-payment problems by the end of 2009. In response, several international rating agencies downgraded the Greek debt contributing to a worsening economic condition of the country. In the beginning of 2010, the fiscal deficit exceeded 1 per cent of Greek GDP, and the country's public debt reached 142 per cent of its GDP. Greece owed over €150 billion to foreign lenders and was unable to continue making interest payments on the outstanding debt. In January 2010, the probability of Greek default was estimated at around 90 per cent. In case of default, it was estimated that losses of the creditors could reach 50 per cent of invested capital. Moreover, despite Greek GDP constituting only a small share of the EU output, Greek financial problems turned into a serious threat to the credibility of the European single currency.[7]

Since May 2010, Greece and other heavily indebted European countries have introduced several austerity measures. These developments were accompanied by efforts undertaken by European authorities as well as international organisations to curb fiscal deficits in the remaining Eurozone Member States, coordinate their fiscal policies and prevent the Eurofrom collapsing. The rescue package prepared for Greece by the EU and the International Monetary Fund (IMF) comprised of €110 billion spread over the three consecutive years in order to stabilise this country. In addition to the Greek bailout, the European Council adopted the European Stabilisation Mechanism in May 2010, which sought to provide additional liquidity to EU Member States threatened by the debt crisis.[8] It is noteworthy that donors to the IMF package included countries like China and India. India's support for the Eurozone rescue package was based on the assumption that negative consequences related to a sovereign default within Europe and fall of a major international currency might be more costly for India than providing additional liquidity for bankrupt EU Member States.[9]

The current crisis in the Eurozone is not – contrary to a common belief – a currency crisis of the Euro, but above all a sovereign debt crisis. A currency crisis can be defined as a sudden decline in confidence in a given currency and its subsequent depreciation.[10] This has not happened to the European single currency. Since the beginning of the crisis in late 2009, the exchange rate of the Euro against the US Dollar has not shown abnormal volatility and the Eurozone interest rates have remained low. The Euro has been losing value against the US Dollar and other international currencies rather slowly.[11] Markets seem to maintain faith in Euro due to well measured actions of the European Central Bank and the weakening position of the American currency.[12] Moreover, as the result of the adoption of the new fiscal treaty – the Fiscal Compact – adopted in March 2012, the Euro has appreciated against the Dollar. (Figure 10.1) Unfortunately, this trend has been reversed by the results of elections in Greece in May and June 2012 and the fear of the country retreating from agreed reforms. Even the improving situation in Italy and other PIIGS cannot outweigh this effect. Figure 1 shows the exchange rate of Euro against the dollar since the beginning of the debt crisis.[13]

Nevertheless, the Eurozone debt crisis has not ceased to be a major problem in the global financial system. Even though the Euro is relatively strong, most European countries have had to face some austerity measures. With a growing debt burden, a country has to shift a large share of its budget spending towards interest payments. This results in less expenditure on the welfare of the citizens and austerity measures inclusive higher taxation.[14] Even if austerity and stabilisation measures prove successful, the economic slowdown in Europe is bound to continue, and adversely affect other regions through trade and financial channels. The countries most hit by the possible recession in Europe could include its major economic partners like India.[15] Moreover, the outstanding government debt in the Eurozone is over €1 trillion to be paid in 2012. For some countries, keeping these obligations might – despite austerity measures – prove impossible.[16] Moreover, there is an on-going debate on the future of the European Union itself since the debt crisis has revealed many political and economic limitations of its current structure.[17] In light of the current speculation on Greece exiting the Eurozone, one must not forget that such an operation would bring additional costs of reintroduction of the national currency. Moreover, the Greek debt would remain denominated in Euro, and even an outright default by this country is not likely to be on its total debt.[18]

Figure 10.1: Rate of Exchange of Euro vis-à-vis the US Dollar, 2009-12

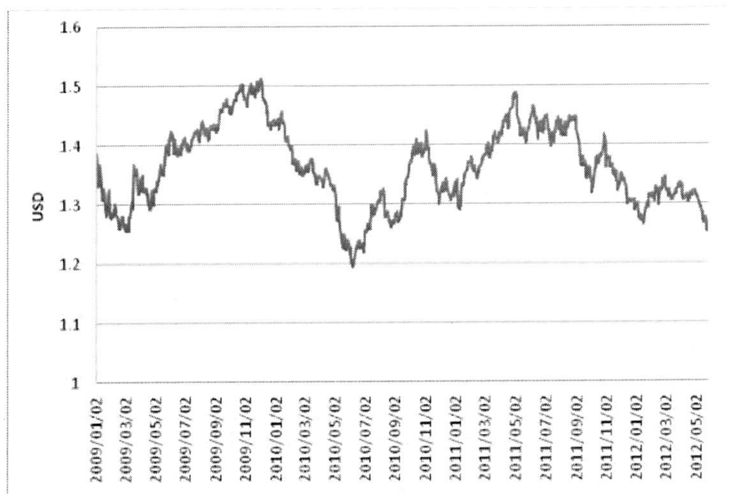

Source: European Central Bank, online: http://www.ecb.int/stats/exchange/eurofxref/html/eurofxref-graph-inr.en.html (accessed 28 May 2012).

Despite European debt-servicing difficulties, growth rates of most Asian economies remain robust. This positive trend can be attributed to high private savings and investment rates accompanied by increasing domestic consumption. Moreover, intra-regional trade in Asia continues to grow and substitutes for trade with weakened European economies. On the other hand, most Asian economies are export-oriented. In these circumstances, even a small decrease in European demand may contribute to an economic slowdown. This effect can already be seen in China, and it will probably affect Korea and Taiwan as well.[19]

The sovereign debt crisis in the Eurozone can also affect Asia through the financial channel. European banks have reduced their credit activity and tried to decrease their exposure in response to a possible default in the Eurozone. The European banking sector will be hit severely by a Greek or Italian default since it possesses a significant amount of bonds issued by these countries. This could lead to an outflow of portfolio capital from Asia since European investors seek to recall resources back to Europe. The same behaviour can be observed from Foreign Institutional Investors (FIIs). Moreover, the tightening of credit policies in Europe are likely to negatively affect foreign direct investment in Asia. European companies will face lower supply and higher cost of capital for investment which may lead to change of plans for investment abroad.[20]

Indian Economy before and after the 2008 Subprime Crisis

The first decade of the new millennium appeared to be highly successful for the Indian economy. The Indian GDP almost doubled and the per capita income exceeded US$3,500 (Purchasing Power Parity) in 2010. Exports were increasing by almost 20 per cent every year (Figure 10.2), and foreign exchange reserves were second only to China.[21] These positive developments were accompanied by a growing integration of India with global markets, and India was included in the group of most promising economies of the world.[22]

Figure 10.2: Indian Exports and Imports, 2002-11

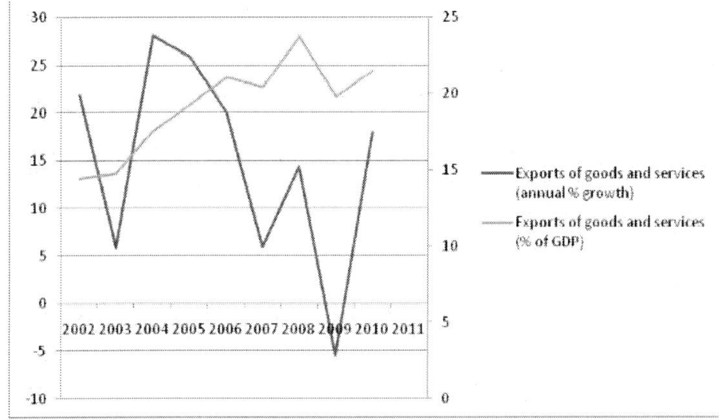

Source: World Bank, 'World Development Indicators& Global Development Finance', online: http://data.worldbank.org/ (accessed 28 May 2012).

Positive Indian growth rates over the past decade have been adversely affected. First, the global subprime crisis hit the Indian financial sector, and affected the real economy. Even though the Indian economy seemed to be slowing down already before 2008, there were still good reasons for optimism. In the first months of 2008, the Indian economy boasted strong macroeconomic fundamentals – inflation was low, economic growth robust, budget deficit declining, export earnings and foreign capital inflows increasing. All these factors led to a high foreign exchange reserves and relatively low foreign debt. Moreover, Indian banks – previously criticised for their limited links with the international financial market – turned out to be in an advantageous position with a very low exposure to toxic assets.[23]

Nevertheless, the impact of the financial crisis on India was more severe than expected. Export growth was temporarily stopped, there was a significant outflow of portfolio capital, and credit supply shrank. There was also a negative impact on the stock market which remains dominated by the FIIs such as hedge funds or pension funds. Property prices started falling and the Indian Rupee began to depreciate quickly despite intervention by the Reserve Bank of India (RBI). These developments led to a contraction of Indian GDP growth from 9 per cent in 2007 to less than 7 per cent in 2008 (Figure 10.3).[24]

Figure 10.3: Indian GDP and GDP Growth Rate, 2002-10

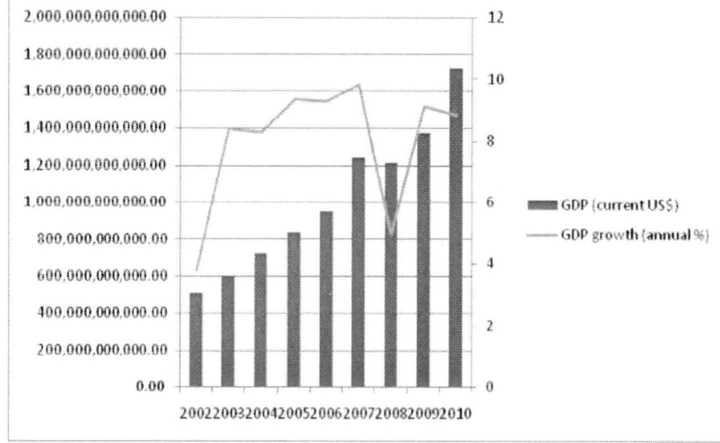

Source: World Bank, 'World Development Indicators & Global Development Finance', online: http://data.worldbank.org/ accessed 28 May 2012.

The effect of the crisis on India proved to be temporary. The Indian economy returned to its growth trajectory in the middle of 2010. Export earnings and capital inflows again increased, thereby contributing to the replenishment of foreign exchange reserves. Even though the effects of the subprime crisis on the Indian economy were not long-lasting, the crisis has uncovered some vulnerabilities in the Indian financial and economic system that might be significant in the current situation. They include insufficient investment in infrastructure, low expenditure on health and education, persisting budget deficit, limited access to credit and, above all, disparities in development between regions.[25]

Today India faces further problems originating in its developed trading and financial sectors. Another constant threat to the Indian economy lies in growing food prices and high commodity costs. International organizations like the IMF and the Asian Development Bank recently reduced India's GDP growth rate projection for the fiscal year ending 31 March 2012. It is estimated that India will grow by less than 7 per cent during 2011-2012 and 2012-2013. It is however not clear to what extent the economic slowdown can be traced back to the Eurozone debt problems.[26] According to many sources, one of the reasons for the current situation is Indian monetary policy during the subprime crisis. Pumping liquidity into the system instead of using fiscal policy tools to stimulate economy seemed to have been insufficient in fighting recession.[27]

One of major factors to have a negative impact on Indian economic growth in recent months has been the constant depreciation of the Rupee. Owing to, *inter alia,* the movement of the Euro against the US Dollar, the Rupee is witnessing high volatility, which, in turn, is affecting the export competitiveness of the country.[28] During 2011, the Rupee has depreciated by

Figure 10.4: Exchange Rates of Indian Rupee vis-à-vis US Dollar and Euro, 2002-10

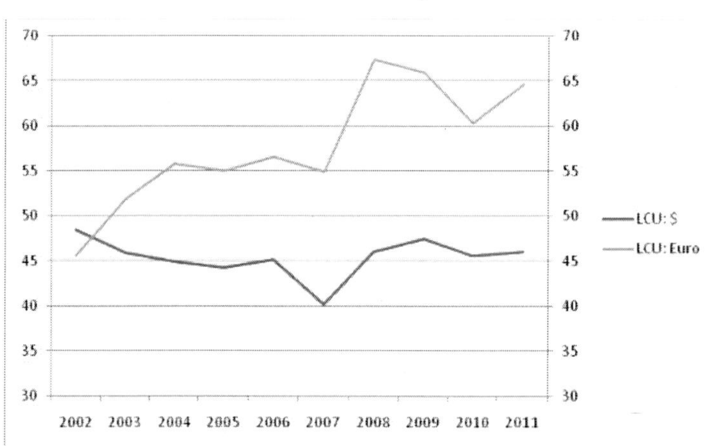

Source: World Bank, Global Economic Prospects, online: http:// data.worldbank.org/ (accessed 28 May 2012).

over 20 per cent against both the US Dollar and the Euro (Figure 10.4). The Rupee has been depreciating despite the country's foreign exchange reserves of almost US$300 billion. Moreover, the Reserve Bank of India's tight interest rate policy has affected growth. The impact has been especially felt in the Indian manufacturing sector.[29]

Exchange rate movements have also led to both negative and positive effects of the Eurozone crisis on India. The depreciating Rupee is likely to add further pressure on domestic inflation and India's import bills. Rupee depreciation will particularly hit the industrial sector and put greater pressure on the cost of items like oil, imported coal, metals and minerals. However, the IT services sector, the textile sector and other export-oriented industries in India are likely to benefit from the depreciating currency.[30]

Impact of the Debt Crisis in the Euro Area on India-EU Trade Relations

Trade is one of the major channels through which economic crises spread to other economies. As the Eurozone countries are among the world's biggest exporters and importers, any changes in demand and terms of trade in the region are immediately reflected in economies of its trading partners. Austerity packages introduced by most European economies have led to reduced public spending which negatively influences growth. Moreover, the depreciation of the Euro and a growing unemployment within the EU has contributed to reduced demand on goods and services imported to Europe.[31] Despite the strong growth of the exports in recent years, India remains a relatively domestic-oriented economy with the share of exports to its GDP averaging around 20 per cent for the last five years when compared to either China or Germany. (Figure 2)[32] Since Indian independence, European countries were among major destinations for Indian exports, and, despite changes in Indian trade policy, the EU still accounts for a significant share of its exports. With almost bilateral trade of US$100 billion (almost €80 billion) in 2011, the EU remains India's major trading partner, but its share in Indian trade is declining.[33] On the other hand, EU-27 exports to India constituted 2.6 per cent of the EU total exports outside the Member States which gives only India eighth position as the EU trading partner.[34]

Indian exports are quite well diversified across countries. Seventeen countries of the Eurozone contribute to less than 15 per cent of India's exports. Of these, the Netherlands (2.1 per cent), Germany (2.7 per cent), Belgium (2.5 per cent), France (2.0 per cent), Italy (1.8 per cent) and Spain (1.0 per cent) contributed to about 13 per cent of the India's exports in 2011. This means that India's exposure to countries most endangered by a default remains relatively low.[35] India also exports mainly non-agricultural products such as machinery and transport equipment, textiles, pharmaceutical products and jewellery to Europe. These sectors have remained relatively unaffected by the crisis. According to the Ministry of Commerce and Industry, Indian exports to EU Member States – both within and outside the Eurozone – has grown by almost 30 per cent in 2011. (Figure 10.5) This indicates – that at least until recently – there has been no negative influence of the European financial distress on trade relations with India.[36]

The depreciation of the Rupee is another factor that might adversely affect Indian trade and contribute to a growing current account deficit. The Indian economy could also be faced with a problem of higher inflation caused by high prices of imported commodities and food products. On the other hand, software services and other export-oriented sectors could benefit from the depreciation of the Rupee.[37]

Figure 10.5: India Trade Balance with EU-27, 2007-11

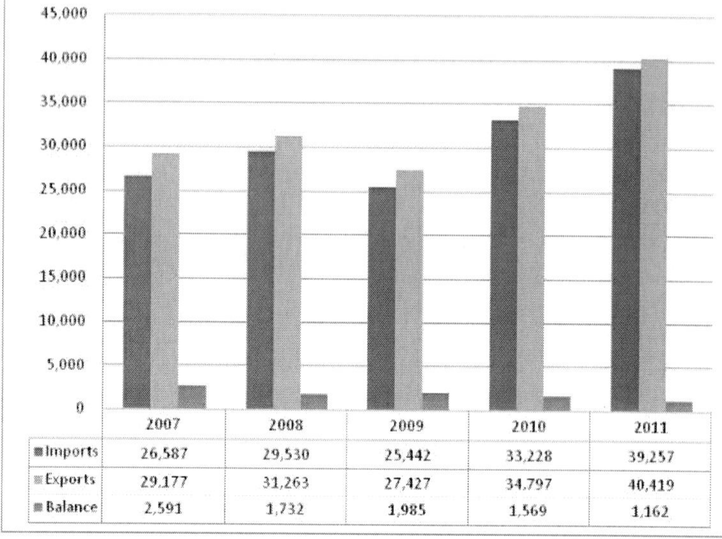

Source: European Commission, *India*, online (downloaded via Eurostat): http://trade.ec.europa.eu/doclib/docs/2006/september/tradoc_113390.pdf (accessed 28 May 2012).

Impact on the Indian Financial Sector

Financial contagion from the Eurozone crisis may occur in the form of spillover through financial intermediaries and stock markets, or changes in investor perception of risks and subsequent modifications of their investment strategies. Eurozone financial problems have been contributing to an increased volatility in global stock markets. This volatility has affected most forms of capital flows around the globe, especially capital inflow to developing countries.[38]

In general, Asian banks can be considered as relatively immune to the European debt problems. It is estimated that only 5 per cent of the European banks' total foreign assets are allocated in the Asia-Pacific region. On the other hand, the high level of uncertainty in financial markets has led to a capital flight from emerging markets. Many Asian banks, as stated earlier, have sought to decrease their financial exposure by selling assets in order to remit cash over to their European headquarters.[39]

These negative developments have also influenced Indian financial markets. As Asian banks are generally not considered as having significant holdings of European sovereign bonds, they are also not considered to be directly threatened by the Eurozone debt crisis. This applies also to the Indian banking system. According to the State Bank of India's Managing Director, A. Krishna Kumar, the exposure of Indian banks to the Eurozone is negligible.[40] It does not mean, however, that the Indian economy will not be negatively affected by the European debt turmoil. Even though the banking system might remain relatively safe, India will suffer from negative changes in investment flows, risk-averse behaviour of institutional investors and reduced value of remittance flows. Moreover, Indian private and public entities might face higher cost of capital in international markets.[41]

Foreign Direct Investment

The high level of financial market distress originating from the Eurozone sovereign debt crisis is deterring investment flows to emerging markets in general.[42] Europe is an important investor in the world economy with EU Foreign Direct Investment (FDI) outflows accounting for over 30 per cent share of global FDI in 2010.[43] European FDI in India has increased between the end of 2008 and the end of 2009 by 56 per cent. Initially this upward tendency continued despite the debt crisis, but eventually FDI inflows from the EU to India declined from €3.4 billion in 2009 to €3 billion in 2010. The most significant European investors in India are Germany, Great Britain and France. These economies – and most notably the private sector in these countries – show positive growth prospects, making negative effects of the debt crisis on European FDI to India seem only temporal.[44]

Moreover, the Eurozone countries in distress, such as Italy, Spain or Greece together contribute a marginal share of less than 1.5 per cent of European FDI flows to India. Hence, it can be assumed that the Eurozone crisis and recession in some countries would not have a significant impact on the Indian economy.[45]

There is also another side of this argument. Europe is becoming an important destination for cross-border investments and overseas acquisitions for Indian companies, including prominent investment in automotive and steel industry.[46] Nevertheless, India's investment into the EU has also reported a decline from €0.9 billion in 2009 to €0.6 billion in 2010. This decline can be attributed to the Eurozone crisis, but in its origins there are high commodity prices and depreciating Rupee as well. Again, these developments seem short-term, as more Indian companies announce their investment plans for the coming months. These actions are similar to activities by major Chinese Sovereign Wealth Funds (SWFs) investing in the European companies taking advantage of the fall in share prices.[47]

Behaviour of Foreign Institutional Investors

If the debt crisis in Europe persists, it will affect investment strategies of institutional investors such as hedge funds, insurance companies, pension funds and mutual funds. Due to the expected decline in stock markets, Foreign Institutional Investors have already started withdrawing their money from emerging markets and turning towards less risky – mostly US dollar-denominated – securities. As most of the FIIs cannot be directly traced back to a particular country, it is hard to assess how the Eurozone crisis affected FII investments in India or any other emerging market. Nevertheless, India experienced a noticeable FII capital outflow in the course of the subprime crisis.[48] Moreover, one of the main drivers of Rupee depreciation since 2009 has been the withdrawal of funds by FIIs from the Indian economy. The share of India's FIIs in the emerging and developing markets has declined from almost 20 per cent in 2010 to less than 4 per cent in 2011 as a consequence of the global slowdown. It is however disputable as to what extent changes in FII behaviour are affected by the Eurozone crisis.[49]

Remittance flows

India is the top recipient of remittance flows. The remittance inflows to India in 2010 are assumed to have exceeded US$55 billion. (Figure 10.6) This means that remittance flows constitute a major source of private foreign financing for India. Yet these numbers are expected to drop by the end of 2012, which may further contribute to the Indian economic slowdown.[50]

Figure 10.6: Remittances to India, 2002-10

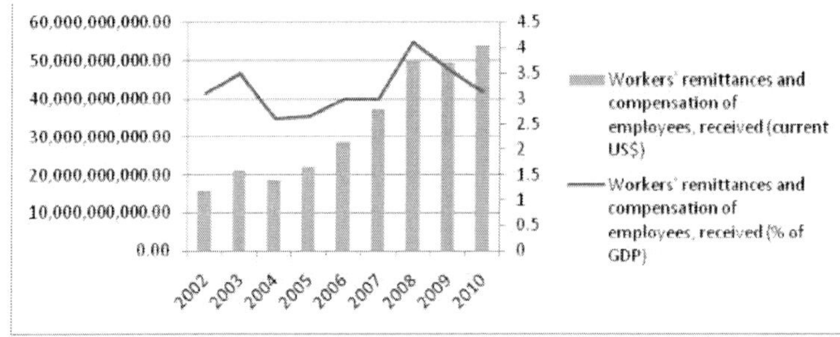

Source: World Bank, 'World Development Indicators & Global Development Finance', online: http://data.worldbank.org/accessed 28 May 2012.

Due to fiscal problems, unemployment in most European economies has been rising for the last two years. The Euro area unemployment rate reached 10 per cent in August 2011, with Spanish unemployment rate exceeding 20 per cent and Irish statistics showing unemployment rate of almost 15 per cent. Negative developments in the labour market translate into reduced income in most categories of workers, including migrant workers. This means lower remittance transfer as immigrants struggle to maintain or find new jobs. A weaker

Euro is also likely to reduce the value of remittances originating from Europe and flowing to developing countries, including India. On the other hand, the PIIGS countries are not among major migration destination from India and the major remittance corridors to India – such as remittance flows from the oil-exporting Gulf countries – seem unaffected.[51]

Foreign exchange reserves

India, as stated earlier, is one of the countries with large foreign exchange reserves. According to the RBI, Indian reserves exceeded US$290 billion in May 2012. As the majority of Indian reserves is denominated in US Dollars, the effect of the debt crisis in Europe is only limited. However, in view of the growing American debt, a strong European currency could provide a good alternative. It is worth mentioning that even though Indian foreign exchange reserves seem to have increased since December 2011, it has actually decreased by almost $7 billion due to the depreciation of the US Dollar.[52] This is the major reason why India, together with China and other emerging economies, is interested in helping Eurozone overcome financial and political difficulties. Moreover, the final effect of the debt crisis in the Euro area on Euro exchange rate and Indian foreign exchange reserves will depend on further developments in major European debtors.[53]

Conclusion

As EU Member States are India's key trade partners, the near future might witness a minor decline in Indian exports due to the lower demand in Europe. On the other hand, Indian exports to European problem debtors like Greece or Italy remains low. Moreover, India exports to the EU mainly non-agricultural products from sectors that were not significantly affected by the crisis. As for the capital flows, there could be a further slowdown in the European FDI inflow to India. This negative effect could be increased by the outflow of portfolio capital.

These factors combined with inflationary pressure within the country and a weak position of the Indian Rupee might lead to a further slowdown in the Indian growth rate. Nevertheless, the European public debt problems seem to have only limited impact on India so far.

The issues described in this chapter unfortunately do not examine all the possible impacts of the Eurozone debt crisis on the Indian economy. Further research is needed on such issues as the influence of the Eurozone crisis on Indian foreign exchange holdings and the possible creation of a Indian sovereign wealth fund, the Indian banking sector and sovereign borrowing, or portfolio flows. Moreover, the Eurozone debt distress contributes to a change in the international financial architecture. Emerging economies, including India, play an increasingly important role in the global economic and financial systems, and the crisis within the Eurozone may strengthen their position as creditors and investors.

NOTES

1 European Commission, *Annual Growth Survey 2012. Communication form the Commission*, Brussels, 23 November 2011, online: http://ec.europa.eu/europe2020/pdf/ags2012_en.pdf (accessed 26 February 2012).

2 "Europe crisis can affect Indian economy," *Hindustan Times*, 13 November 2011, online: http://www.hindustantimes.com/business-news/WorldEconomy/Europe-crisis-can-affect-Indian-economy-Pranab/Article1-768633.aspx (accessed 26 February 2012).

3 There is no single definition of sovereign default. From a legal point of view, a sovereign default is a situation when a scheduled debt service is not paid beyond a grace period specified in the debt contract. Next, any episode in which the sovereign makes a restructuring offer that contains terms less favourable than the original debt is usually interpreted as an indication of debt-servicing difficulties and, therefore, a default. Marcel Peter, "Estimating Default Probabilities of Emerging Market Sovereigns: A New Look at a Not-So-New Literature," *HEI Working Paper, No. 06-2002*, p. 8.

4 William R. Cline, *International Debt Reexamined* (Washington D.C.: Institute for International Economics, 1995), p. 14; Federico Sturzenegger and Jeromin Zettelmeyer, *Debt Defaults and Lessons from a Decade of Crises* (Cambridge, Mass.: The MIT Press, 2006), p. ix.

5 A bailout involves the International Monetary Fund (IMF), and other multilateral organisations providing sufficient funds to make that country able to continue servicing its debt. Paulo A. De Britto, "Sovereign Debt: Default, Market Sanction, and Bailout," *Econometric Society 2004 Latin American Meetings*, No. 237/2004, p. 2.

6 Isabella Massa, Jodie Keane, Jane Kennan, "The Eurozone Crisis: Risks for Developing Countries," *ODI Background Note*, October 2011, p. 1.

7 Mohamed El-Erian, "Why the Greek rescue isn't going to plan," *Financial Times*, 7 April 2010; Tony Czuczka and John Glover, "Greece Default Push Risks Reviving Contagion as Bonds Plunge," *Bloomberg Businessweek*, 19 April 2011, online: http://www.businessweek.com/news/2011-04-19/greece-default-push-risks-reviving-contagion-as-bonds-plunge.html (accessed 26 February 2012); Marek Dabrowski, "Euro Crisis or Debt Crisis," *CASE Network E-briefs*, No 09/2010, June 2010.

8 Michael G. Arghyrou, AlexandrosKontonikas, "The EMU Sovereign-Debt Crisis: Fundamentals, Expectations and Contagion," *European Economy Economic Papers*, No. 436, February 2011, p. 3; European Union, *The European Stabilization Mechanism*, Brussels, May 2010, online: http://europa.eu/rapid/pressReleasesAction.do? reference=MEMO/10/173 (accessed 26 February 2012).

9 "India to give $2bn to fund bailouts in Europe," *The Times of India*, 3 August 2011, online: http://articles.timesofindia.indiatimes.com/2011-08-03/india/29846212_1_bailouts-economies-debt-crisis (accessed 26 February 2012).

10 Dabrowski, n. 7.

11 Massa, n. 6, p. 1.

12 European Central Bank, online: http://www.ecb.int/stats/exchange/eurofxref/html/eurofxref-graph-usd.en.html (accessed 26 February 2012).

13 European Council, *Treaty on Stability, Coordination and Governance in the Economic and Monetary Union*, online: http://www.european-council.europa.eu/media/639235/st00tscg26_en12.pdf (accessed 28 May 2012).

14 Shubha Ganesh, "Eurozone debt crisis to remain a concern in the near future," *Economic Times*, 11 December 2011.

15 Shuvojit Banerjee, "The European debt crisis: implications for Asia and the Pacific," *MPDD Policy Briefs*, No. August 2010, pp. 3-4.
16 Ganesh, n. 14.
17 Yeo Lay Hwee, Tommy Koh, "Light at the end of Euro Tunnel," *The Straits Times*, 14 Mar 2012, online: http://www.eucentre.sg/details.php?i=29 (accessed 28 May 2012).
18 Dabrowski, n. 7.
19 Ranjan Chakravarty, Joseph Cherian, "The Nagging Eurozone Crisis and its Implications," National University of Singapore, November 2011, online: http://www.bschool.nus.edu/Portals/0/images/CAMRI/Thought per cent20Leadership/The per cent20nagging per cent20Eurozone per cent20crisis per cent20and per cent20its per cent20implications.pdf (accessed 26 February 2012).
20 Chakravarty, n. 19.
21 World Bank, online: http://siteresources.worldbank.org/DATASTATISTICS/Resources/GNIPC.pdf (accessed 26 February 2012).
22 Utsav Kumar and Arvind Subramanian, "India's Growth in the 2000s: Four Facts," *Peterson Institute for International Economics Working Paper Series*, WP 11-17, November 2011; Goldman Sachs, online http://www.goldmansachs.com/our-thinking/global-economic-outlook/the-growth-map/index.html (accessed 26 February 2012).
23 Joachim Betz, "India and the International Financial Crisis," Paper presented to the IPSA-Conference in Sao Paolo, "Whatever Happened to North-South," February 2011, p. 1.
24 On the effects of the financial crisis on Asian economies, see Morris Goldstein and Daniel Xie, "The Impact of the Financial Crisis on Emerging Asia," *Peterson Institute for International Economics Working Paper Series*, WP 09-11, October 2009; Betz, n. 23, pp. 4-5; Impact of Global Financial Crisis on South Asia, South Asia Region, The World Bank Group, online: http://siteresources.worldbank.org/SOUTHASIAEXT/Resources/223546-1171488994713/3455847-1232124140958/gfcsouthasiafeb172009.pdf, p. 2 (accessed 28 May 2012).
25 Betz, n. 23, pp. 1-2.
26 International Monetary Fund, *World Economic Outlook Update. Global Recovery Stalls, Downside Risks Intensify*, 24 January 2012, online: http://www.imf.org/external/pubs/ft/weo/2012/update/01/ (accessed 28 May 2012).
27 "Eurozone debt crisis to have limited impact on India's economy,

banking sector," *Contify Banking*, 13 October 2011, online: http://banking.contify.com/story/indian-economy-and-banking-sector-may-remain-unaffected-with-european-sovereign-debt-crisis-says-sbi-md-kumar-2011-10-13 (accessed on 26 February 2012); Rajiv Kumar Bhatt, "Recent Global Meltdown and its Impact on Indian Economy," *2011 International Conference on Economics, Trade and Development*, *IPEDR*, vol. 7 (2011), Singapore, p. 93.

28 "India would be impacted by 'prolonged' Euro Debt Crisis," *The Hindu Business Line*, 13 November 2011, online: http://www.thehindubusinessline.com/industry-and-economy/economy/article2624374.ece (accessed 26 February 2012).

29 Chakravarty and Cherian, n. 19, p. 1; Peter Boone, and Simon Johnson, "The European Crisis Deepens," *Peterson Institute for International Economics Policy Brief*, Number PB12-4, January 2012; "Indian Rupee depreciation 2012: Causes, Concerns and Future Outlook," *CARE Limited*, online: http://indiamicrofinance.com/indian-Rupee-depreciation-2012.html (accessed 26 February 2012).

30 "Impact of Euro Crisis and Global Slowdown on India," *CARE Ratings*, December 2011, p. 8.

31 Massa *et al.*, n. 6, pp. 2-3.

32 "Impact of Euro Crisis and Global Slowdown on India," n. 30, p. 1.

33 Gulshan Sachdeva, "The Eurozone Crisis and India-EU Ties," *IDSA Comment*, 7 February 2012, online: http://www.idsa.in/idsacomments/TheEurozoneCrisisandIndia EUTies_gsacjdeva_ 070212 (accessed 26 February 2012).

34 Eurostat, online: http://ec.europa.eu/trade/creating-opportunities/bilateral-relations/countries/india/index_en.htm (accessed 28 May 2012).

35 "Impact of Euro Crisis and Global Slowdown on India," n. 30, pp. 1 and 4.

36 India, Ministry of Commerce and Industry, Department of Commerce, http://commerce.nic.in/eidb/ergncnt.asp (accessed 26 February 2012).

37 "Impact of Euro Crisis and Global Slowdown on India," n. 30, pp. 1 and 5.

38 Massa *et al.*, n. 6, p. 2; Chakravarty and Cherian, n. 19, p. 1.

39 Gnès Bénassy-Quéré, et al., "Don't let the euro-are crisis go east," *Asia-Europe Economic Forum Paper*, January 2012, pp. 1-2.

40 Banerjee, n. 15, p. 4. "Euro zone debt crisis to have limited impact on India's economy, banking sector."

41 As for now private investors do not punish Asian markets for its. See Banerjee, n. 15, p. 2.
42 "How Will the Eurozone Crisis Affect Asia in 2012?", *Ernst & Young,* 16 December 2011.
43 Massa *et al.*, n. 6, p. 3.
44 "Impact of Euro Crisis and Global Slowdown on India," p. 6; Eurostat, http://epp.eurostat.ec.europa.eu/statistics_explained/index.php/Foreign_direct_investment_statistics (accessed 26 February 2012); Sachdeva, n. 33.
45 "Impact of Euro Crisis and Global Slowdown on India," p. 7.
46 Sachdeva, n. 33.
47 "Private equity owner to sell Ducati," online: http://www.reuters.com/article/2012/02/13/us-ducati-sale-idUSTRE81C0VV20120213 (accessed 26 February 2012).
48 Bhatt, n. 27, p. 93.
49 "Impact of Euro Crisis and Global Slowdown on India," pp. 7-8.
50 The World Bank, *Migration and Remittances Factbook 2011*, Second Edition, Washington D.C. 2011, online http://siteresources. worldbank.org/INTLAC/Resources/Factbook2011-Ebook.pdf, p. 138 (accessed on 28 May 2012).
51 Massa *et al.*, n. 6, p. 3; "How the Eurozone Debt Crisis could affect Developing Countries," *The Guardian*, 21 October 2011, online: http://www.guardian.co.uk/global-development/poverty-matters/2011/oct/21/eurozone-crisis-developing-countries (accessed 26 February 2012).
52 Reserve Bank of India, Weekly Statistical Supplement, online: http://rbidocs.rbi.org.in/rdocs/Wss/PDFs/02T_250512S.pdf (accessed 28 May 2012).
53 Bénassy-Quér et al., n. 39, p. 2.

11

Climate Change: India and the European Union

Archna Negi

"Recognizing *that climate change represents an urgent and potentially irreversible threat to human societies and the planet and thus requires to be urgently addressed by all Parties, and acknowledging that the global nature of climate change calls for the widest possible cooperation by all countries and their participation in an effective and appropriate international response, with a view to accelerating the reduction of global greenhouse gas emissions...*"

[Durban, South Africa, 2011][1]

Introduction

The recently held United Nations Climate Change Conference at Durban (2011)[2] has been described as having "delivered a breakthrough".[3] One of the significant outcomes of the conference is the decision to adopt a legal agreement on climate change that will come into force no later than 2020. The novelty of the new agreement will be its aim to set up a common legal framework for both developed and developing countries. The agreement comes after a history of deep divergences and scratching the surface will reveal the fissures that exist amongst the international community on the issue of climate change. Although there is widespread recognition of the need for urgent and systematic action, sharp differences continue to exist regarding burden allocation. Previous climate change negotiations have showcased these differences and the failure to achieve expected results[4] at Copenhagen in December 2009[5] is still fresh in public memory. It will be interesting to see whether long-standing differences in negotiating stances can be overcome to meet the 2020 deadline.

Despite the recognized 'global' nature of the problem, efforts to combat climate change are not limited to the international level; regional, bilateral, national and local initiatives seek to contribute to the overall effort to address the concern. Both India and the European Union (EU) are important players in the climate change debate. The EU has been one of the leading historical contributors to the current carbon stock but it has also displayed a serious commitment to contribute to the efforts to address the problem. It has consciously prioritized the issue of climate change and has initiated action at all levels – international, regional and domestic – to put in place policies to combat climate change. India, with its overwhelming population, growing economy and development needs, has also joined the ranks of the big emitters in absolute terms, although it has consistently underscored at international fora its low per capita emissions. At the national level, too, it has initiated policies to promote low-carbon growth. Both actors have an important role to play in the international negotiations on climate change and both have also taken action at the domestic level to combat climate change. Climate change has also emerged as one of the prominent issues of concern in the bilateral strategic relations between EU and India.

This chapter attempts an analysis of the issue of climate change at three different levels, each of which involves the two identified actors. Section 2 focuses on the role of the EU and India in the international climate change regime. Under this regime, comprising the United Nations Framework Convention on Climate Change, 1992 (UNFCCC) and its Kyoto Protocol, 1997, both India and the EU have an important role etched out for them. The recent clash between the EU and India at the Durban Climate Conference in December 2011 over the legal status of the possible new global agreement highlighted the difference in approaches between the two. In this section, convergences and divergences between these two actors – EU and India – in the context of the international climate change regime are sought to be identified. The possible roles of both actors in the post-Kyoto scenario are explored in this section.

Section 3 of the chapter analyses the initiatives undertaken by both EU and India individually at the domestic level. The European Commission has been involved in efforts relating to climate change since 1991, when it adopted its first strategy to limit CO_2 emissions. Since then, several Directives have been undertaken and in June 2000, the Commission launched the European Climate Change Programme (ECCP) in order to develop an EU strategy to implement the Kyoto Protocol. Subsequently, the second ECCP was launched in 2005. The policy package adopted in December 2008 represented a big step forward in strengthening action for climate change. While the EU has put stringent mechanisms in place in relation to mitigation and adaptation, recognizing climate change as a *security threat*, India has also recently initiated action on climate change at the national level, with the formulation of the National Action Plan on Climate Change in June 2008. The perceptions and implications of climate change are vastly different in Europe and in India and these distinctions could help explain divergences in policy at the domestic level.

Current and potential collaborative bilateral efforts between the EU and India on climate change are discussed in Section 4. Among the major global challenges addressed at the annual EU-India summits since 2000, climate change has held a prominent place. How far can the commonality of values, beliefs and commitments that underlie the 'strategic partnership' between the EU and India be successfully extended to combating climate change? The EU-India Joint Action Plan of 2008 refers to India and EU as "global partners for global challenges"; this section examines the potential of this partnership to address the global challenge of climate change.

Section 5 contains general conclusions. The chapter is premised on the understanding that the issue of climate change will continue to grow in importance and pervade other policy spaces as well. The choice of the two actors that are central to this study is self-evident considering their undeniable significance in any architecture designed to combat climate change.

International Climate Change Regime: EU and India

The international climate change regime is embodied in UNFCCC, 1992, which has the twin objectives of stabilizing greenhouse gas (GHG) concentrations in the atmosphere to a safe level (*mitigation*) and coping with temperature rise (*adaptation*).[6] The 1997 Kyoto Protocol to the UNFCCC, which was to cover the time period till 2012, contains specific obligations to be undertaken by parties, including binding emission reduction targets that were imposed on some parties (Annex I).[7] Of the 192 parties to the Protocol, 37 industrialized states and the European Community committed to reducing GHG emissions [by an average of 5 per cent against 1990 levels over the five-year period (2008-2012)].[8] The defining feature of the climate regime – and also what makes it most controversial – is that it is based on the principle of 'common but differentiated responsibilities', i.e. it recognizes that the developed countries are principally responsible for current GHG stock in the atmosphere (emitted in 150-200 years of industrial activity) and therefore places a higher burden on them.[9] While industrial countries are to meet their reduction targets first and foremost by taking domestic action, the Protocol allows the meeting of emission reduction commitments abroad through market based 'Kyoto/flexibility mechanisms'.[10] Implementing the Kyoto Protocol proved problematic because the emissions reductions that it mandates translate directly into a curtailment of development activities.[11] Despite this, the Protocol entered into force in 2005.

The Stern Review in 2006 analysed the economics of global warming and underscored the enormous costs of failing to act. The review concluded that the benefits of early action on climate change would outweigh the costs of action quite substantially.[12] In 2007, the Intergovernmental Panel on Climate Change (IPCC) brought out its Fourth Assessment Report, [13] establishing that the world could not afford climate change of more than 2 degrees Celsius above the pre-industrial era. The renewed sense of urgency imparted by this report coupled with the impending end of the Kyoto period (2012), led to the adoption of the Bali Action Plan in 2007, according to which an 'agreed outcome' was to be reached by the end of 2009 at Copenhagen.[14]

In December 2009, the Copenhagen conference (COP 15) was held under the weight of the world's expectations to agree to a successor agreement to Kyoto. But there were many sticking points that evaded resolution: By how much were the industrialized countries willing to reduce their emissions by 2020 (mid-term commitments)? What steps were the developing countries (in particular, the large emerging economies like India and China) willing to take to limit growth of their emissions?[15] To what amount and mode of financing for adaptation and mitigation were the developed countries willing to commit? What commitments relating to technology development and transfer were achievable? While the industrialized countries argued for meaningful participation by emerging economies in any future agreement, the developing countries resisted the imposition of binding commitments and stressed the need for financial and technological support from the developed countries. Although a range of options was thrown up for discussion in relation to these questions, divergences remained both on broad principle as well as on specific detail.

What was achieved at Copenhagen was a non-binding

political statement – the 'Copenhagen Accord', [16] which some viewed favourably as 'an important first step' and others saw as a 'weak outcome' resulting from "a dirty collusive deal between the United States and BASIC (Brazil, South Africa, India and China)".[17] The Copenhagen Accord endorsed the scientific view that temperature increases must be contained to less than 2 degrees Celsius since pre-industrial times.[18] The basic design of the Copenhagen Accord was that each Party committed (in written) to abide by certain listed domestic mitigation commitments ('schedule approach'). While the developed countries were to list 'quantified economy-wide emissions targets for 2020' (Appendix I), developing countries were required to list 'nationally appropriate mitigation actions' (Appendix II). There was a collective commitment on the part of the developed countries for funding to the tune of $30 billion covering both adaptation and mitigation and a further commitment to mobilize $100 billion annually by 2020 from public as well as private sources.

At the COP 17 held in November-December 2011 at Durban, an agreement was reached to have a successor to the Kyoto Protocol to be negotiated by 2015 and to enter into force by 2020. This proposed "legal" agreement is to contain mitigation commitments for *all* UN members. In the meanwhile, the Kyoto Protocol has been extended to a second four-year phase, extending from 2013-2017, during which governments will negotiate the timeframes within which countries should cut emissions. With the US already outside the Kyoto framework, and Japan, Canada and Russia refusing to sign up to a second period, the EU has taken up the solitary responsibility among developed countries of continuing the Kyoto Protocol.

There were differences – most visibly between the EU and India – over the nature of the proposed agreement. The EU Climate Change Commissioner, Connie Hedegaard pointed out that EU was prepared to offer to stay with their Kyoto commitments through a second period provided that was followed by a legally-binding agreement applicable to all countries. "We are almost ready to be alone in a second commitment period [to the Kyoto Protocol]. We don't ask too much of the world that after this second period, all countries will be legally bound."[19] India opposed the introduction of a "legal" agreement, basing its arguments on its traditional reliance on the 'common but differentiated responsibilities' principle. In the much-quoted words of India's Minister for Environment and Forests, Jayanti Natarajan, "Am I to write a blank cheque and sign away the livelihoods and sustainability of 1.2 billion Indians, without even knowing what the EU 'roadmap' contains? I wonder if this is an agenda to shift the blame on to countries who are not responsible [for climate change]."[20] The compromise language arrived at was a commitment to negotiate a protocol, another legal instrument or an "agreed outcome with legal force". Differences over the legal status of the new agreement stem from the fact that the developed countries have long wanted emerging economies like China and India to be legally bound to take action, albeit apportioning them softer emissions reduction targets, while the developing countries point to their self-imposed voluntary targets as adequate given their low historic share in causing the problem.

The "Durban Package" comprises four components: *i)* the Second Commitment Period (SCP) for emissions reduction by Annex I countries under the Kyoto Protocol; *ii)* a decision on the work of the Ad Hoc Working Group on Long-term Cooperative Action (AWG-LCA); *iii)* a decision on the Green Climate Fund (GCF); and *iv)* an agreement on the Durban Platform.[21] Other areas of agreement at Durban included "measures aimed at protecting forests, widening global markets and establishing by 2020 a $100 billion fund to help poorer countries move to a green economy and cope with the effects of climate change".[22]

International Climate Regime and EU

The EU is a significant player in the international climate regime. It (and its then 10 members) ratified the UNFCCC in December 1993 and the Kyoto Protocol in May 2002. The EU has traditionally been a staunch supporter of the Kyoto regime and had played a major role in bringing the Kyoto negotiations to a successful conclusion. As an Annex I entity, the EU had a binding commitment to reduce its GHG emissions by 8 per cent in the first commitment period (2008-2012). EU Member States share this target through a binding, burden-sharing agreement. Post-Durban, the EU remains the only set of developed countries to continue to implement the Kyoto Protocol in the second commitment period.

The EU's involvement in the international climate regime is based on the recognition of the fact that developed countries are responsible for 75 per cent of GHG stock and they have the most financial and technological capabilities to cut emissions. The EU therefore agrees that it (and other developed countries) must take the lead in showing the way forward and unhesitatingly take on binding commitments to reduce emissions. At Copenhagen, the EU had favoured the adoption of a legally binding global treaty that was science-based and that covered all major emitters. It endorsed the quantified objective of limiting global warming to less than 2 degrees Celsius above pre-industrial level.[23] According to the Fourth Assessment Report of the IPCC, reduction of global emissions by half (of 1990) by 2050 would require developed countries to cut their emissions by 25-40 per cent below 1990 levels by 2020 and by 80-95 per cent by 2050. The EU supported these figures and advocated that the developed countries take the lead by making 'deep emission cuts'.[24]

The EU also strongly felt, however, that the emerging economies should pledge 'ambitious, quantified mitigation actions', as developing country emissions are projected to soon overtake emissions from the developed world. It expected developing country pledges to collectively amount to a deviation of 15-30 per cent below currently predicted growth rate by 2020. Reducing emissions from deforestation will have to be part of this effort by the developing countries. The EU's overall proposal is that all developing countries (except the least developed countries) must commit to adopting low-carbon development strategies. In return, the EU stated its willingness to provide financial assistance to developing countries for mitigation and adaptation. The key components of a possible treaty were also worked out by the EU such as a procedure for codifying emission mitigation contributions by both developed and developing counties; targets for reducing global emissions from international aviation and maritime transport sectors; a framework of action on adaptation; a framework for international cooperation on technology; strengthened rules on monitoring, reporting and verification (MRV), etc.[25] At Durban, the EU achieved an important component of its 'roadmap' when it successfully got members to agree to an agreement applying to all by 2015.

The EU has made international commitments to several climate and energy targets and has also taken steps to realize these commitments. At a general level, EU leaders have undertaken to transform Europe, making it a 'highly energy-efficient, low-carbon economy'. In March 2007, EU announced a commitment to cut its emissions to 30 per cent below 1990 levels by 2020, provided other developed countries commit comparably and emerging economies pledge to contribute as per their capabilities. Further, regardless of the action or inaction on the part of other countries, the EU committed to a cut in emissions by at least 20 per cent of 1990 levels by 2020, in order to gain a 'first mover advantage'. These emission reduction targets are supported by 3 energy-related objectives to be met by 2020: *i)* 20 per cent reduction in energy consumption (through efficiency); *ii)* increased share of renewable energy in market (from 9 per cent to 20 per cent); and *iii)* 10 per cent share for sustainably produced biofuels/ renewable fuels in transport.[26] Thus, the EU has undertaken relatively deep commitments relating to mitigation.

International Climate Regime and India

India has ratified the UNFCCC (1 November 1993) as well as the Kyoto Protocol (26 August 2002). Under the Kyoto Protocol, India is a non-Annex I country and therefore is not currently bound by any emissions reduction commitments. However, at Durban, after offering stiff opposition, India finally conceded to the idea of a legal agreement applying to all UN members. India's prominence in the climate change negotiations increased after the US made its subscription to the Kyoto regime contingent upon binding emission reduction commitments by countries like India. India's negotiating position in the climate regime has largely been defined by its response to this argument of the US. The central feature of India's position has been an absolute refusal to be bound by legally binding emission reduction commitments for at least two reasons. As a first justification, India invokes the 'common but differentiated responsibilities' principle that is central to the architecture of the current climate regime. A second defense of its stand comes from a stress on convergence of 'per capita emissions' of developing and developed countries. With the US at roughly 19 and India at only 1.3 (US Department of Energy) in terms of per capita emissions, the Indian Prime Minister could assert confidently, as he did at the G8 Summit at Heiligendamm, Germany in 2007 that India's per capita emission would never exceed that of the developed countries.

At Bangkok in 2009, India stressed that a continuation of the Kyoto Protocol along with deep cuts by the developed countries was non-negotiable. It further stressed that immediate and deep cuts in GHG emissions to be undertaken by the developed countries should be accompanied with specific mid-term targets. On its part, India proposed country-specific 'nationally appropriate mitigation actions' that could be supported with finance and technology and verified. However, it was made clear that India would not agree to any international review (measurement, reporting and verification) of its unilateral and unsupported domestic actions. Another issue argued by the developing countries is that of technology transfer and financing as a repayment of the carbon debt by the developed countries.

India has been proactively involved in the climate negotiations at various international fora. At the Major Economies Forum (G8 + G5 + Australia + EU + Indonesia + South Korea), when India endorsed the "scientific view that increase in global average temperature above pre-industrial levels ought not to exceed 2 degrees Celsius", there was widespread media criticism as this was seen as an admission on an emissions cap. But according to Indian negotiators, this was only a 'political statement of intent' and not an 'arithmetical binding target'. India has shown a keenness to be seen as a proactive participant of the climate regime, not an excessively defensive 'deal-breaker'. As evidence of its increased commitment to the cause of climate change, it has accelerated domestic action, viz. by finalizing its National Action Plan on Climate Change in June 2008. India's keenness to be accommodative was also captured in a controversial letter by the Indian Minister for Environment and Forests, Jairam Ramesh, to the Prime Minister dated 13 October 2009, in which the minister seemed to reverse India's negotiating stance.[27] The letter had raised widespread concern over whether the Indian government was clear about its negotiating strategy.

The Indian position has strongly been tied to the refusal to be bound by binding emissions reduction commitments. Some academic views, although they have not yet been discussed as part of the formal international negotiations, do provide alternatives and merit attention and consideration.

Noted economist, Jagdish Bhagwati[28] draws attention to the fact that while the 'stock problem' (80 per cent of carbon accumulated in the atmosphere has come from the West) has been the point of reference in the climate negotiations, we cannot ignore the 'flow problem' (more than half the current carbon discharge into atmosphere is from the developing countries). He suggests that countries such as China and India should assume flow obligations although these would depend on the fulfillment of stock obligations by the developed countries. He also suggests that acceptance of current obligations would be contingent upon payment for past damages. Acceptance of (binding) flow obligations on the part of developing countries is impossible to imagine in the current state of negotiations but if it did come about at some point in time, it would represent a huge turning point in the climate change negotiations.

Another alternative to help break the deadlock by modifying the negotiating position of India is provided by Raghunandan, Purkayastha and Jayaraman,[29] who suggest that India should announce *non-binding* but *self-declared* targets to restrict emissions to 25 per cent below *projected* emissions by 2030 (rather than an absolute cut in emissions) *conditional upon: i)* Annex I parties meeting binding targets of reducing emissions by 50 per cent below 1990 levels by 2030 and 90 per cent by 2050 (deep cuts through actual reductions not offset through trade measures); *ii)* Annex I countries to pay into a climate fund a sum equivalent to deficit in target achievement *iii)* emission reduction technologies to be placed in public domain. This suggested solution also seeks to acknowledge current responsibility and to include action on the part of developing countries. But the inclusion of developing countries would be contingent on a continued stress on historical responsibility and meaningful action in that direction by the developed countries.

India has always stressed that its refusal to be bound by international reduction commitments in no way implies reluctance on its part to undertake climate-related effort. In December 2009, India announced an intention to cut carbon emission intensity by 20-25 per cent of 2005 levels by 2050.[30] This would be achieved through a combination of measures such as converting to clean coal technology, fuel efficiency standards for the transport sector and a mandatory green building code. However, it was stressed that these measures would be voluntary and that India would not agree to internationally binding commitments. Although averse to international review of domestic mitigation actions, it was announced that the Twelfth Five-Year Plan would focus on low-carbon strategy for growth.

Domestic Policy and Action on Climate Change: EU and India

Both EU and India have undertaken initiatives at the domestic level to combat climate change. The nature of these efforts, however, is vastly different. This is not surprising considering the different points that these actors occupy on the development trajectory and the resulting differences in perception and priority accorded to the issue of climate change. While the EU has long had climate change concerns as a high priority agenda, resulting also in part from the demands of the environmentally-conscious populace, in India, climate change as a policy concern is a new entrant and interest remains limited to a handful of urban elite, policy makers, NGOs and academicians.

EU Action on Climate Change

Climate change action in Europe is taken both at the level of the European Union and at the level of each of the Member States, which individually implement domestic action to complement action at the regional level. The EU Security Strategy of 2003 recognizes global warming as a *security threat* and an EU document published in 2008 sees climate change as a potential 'threat multiplier'.[31] The European Climate

Change Programme (ECCP) represents a set of policy measures to reduce GHG emissions. Launched by the European Commission in 2000, the ECCP aimed at identifying policies and measures for GHG emission reduction at the EU level in order to ensure that the EU could meet its target for emissions reduction under the Kyoto Protocol.[32] The Kyoto commitment for the EU entailed a combined emission cut to 8 per cent below 1990 levels by 2012 by the 15 EU members before 2004. Under the multi-stakeholder consultative process set up by the ECCP, 11 working groups were established to identify options for reducing emissions. One of the most important outcomes of the first ECCP was the EU Emissions Trading Scheme, which covered approximately 11,500 heavy carbon emitters in the power and manufacturing sectors. The Second European Climate Change Programme was initiated in 2005 to further explore cost effective ways of cutting GHG emissions. New working groups were established under the new scheme including carbon capture and storage, adaptation, and emissions by the transport and aviation sector.

The European Union, as stated earlier, has undertaken a commitment to transform Europe into a 'highly energy-efficient, low-carbon economy'. Several measures have been undertaken by the EU to implement its international commitments of March 2007 relating to emissions cuts by at least 20 per cent (and upto 30 per cent) of 1990 levels by 2020. A set of three energy-related objectives complemented the emissions reduction commitments. In January 2008, the European Commission adopted a package of legislative measures to implement these climate- and energy-related targets, which became legally enforceable in April 2009. The adoption of this package makes the EU a leader in committing to ambitious mitigation targets and operationalizing measures to achieve these targets.[33]

The package also involves a revamping of the EU's Emissions Trading Scheme (EU ETS) from 2013 so that it contributes two thirds of the overall emissions reductions intended to be achieved by 2020. The cap on emission allowances will be cut every year 2013 onwards to reduce by 2020 the number of emission allowances available. The ETS scheme will also be broadened to include other big emitting sectors (such as chemicals and aluminum sectors) as well as other emissions (perfluorocarbons). In 2013, national caps on emissions will be replaced by a EU-wide cap. Also, the system of receiving emission allowances for free will be replaced by a system of buying allowances in auction (full auctioning is targeted for 2027). The income generated from auctioning will be used by governments to combat climate change.[34]

Interestingly, the EU implements its own version of the 'common but differentiated responsibilities principle', wherein national emission targets for 2020 are differentiated according to member states' relative per capita GDP. So the targets range from a 20 per cent emissions *reduction* by members such as Denmark and Ireland to a 20 per cent *increase* by Bulgaria. But the poor member states will still need to reduce their emissions from 'business-as-usual' scenarios.[35] A similar differentiation of national targets is implemented for targets relating to the use of renewable energy (the EU target is of obtaining 20 per cent of energy consumption from renewable energy by 2020). The EU climate package also implements a framework for making 'carbon capture and storage' (CCS) technology commercially viable by 2020.[36] The package also has stringent measures to check GHG emissions from the transport sector, which is a special challenge.[37] Also, the R&D budget for environment, energy and transport has been substantially increased to enhance the state of knowledge relating to clean technologies.

The recent EU initiative that has generated a large-scale controversy is to implement a carbon tax to international airlines flying to and from European airspace, starting 2012. The European ETS creates a permit system for carbon emissions in order to incentivize airlines to emit less. Airlines will be allotted permits for carbon emissions and they will have to buy extra permits if they wish to exceed their allocation. Further, the number of permits will be reduced over time. Payments are due from 2013. The European Court of Justice, in December 2011, ruled against US airlines that had contested the EU legislation. This unilateral move to include non-EU airlines into the European ETS has been formally opposed by 26 countries – including China, India, Russia and the US – that met in Moscow in February 2012 to consider possibilities of retaliation. These countries favour a multilateral approach arrived at under the aegis of the International Civil Aviation Organization (ICAO), as decided under the Kyoto Protocol. This controversy is bound to bring to fore the long-standing academic debates over the potential conflict between the Kyoto Protocol and the World Trade Organization rules.

India's Action on Climate Change

The climate change issue is of immense importance for India from the point of view of vulnerability. Not only are many crucial sectors of its largely natural resource based economy – such as agriculture, water and forestry – climate-sensitive but also the large populations of poor that it houses are ill equipped to cope with the adverse impact of climate change.[38]

Several of the existing Indian policies that are aimed at energy efficiency and resource conservation simultaneously address climate change concerns. The National Environment Policy, 2006, the Integrated Energy Policy, 2008 and the Five-Year Plans – all make references to climate change concerns. The National Environment Policy, 2006 identifies climate change as a 'key environmental challenge'.[39] The promotion of renewable energy technology, energy efficiency, etc. by government policies has resulted in a decrease in energy intensity as well as emissions intensity in the last 20 years. One example of India's concern for energy efficiency is embodied in the Energy Conservation Act, 2001, which allows the government to set standards and norms for energy consumption and also to ensure compliance with them. The Act also provides for energy audits, involving verification, monitoring and analysis of energy use and prescribes the preparation of action plans by major commercial consumers to reduce consumption.

Other programmes such as standards and labeling programme for electrical appliances and green rating of buildings initiative also contribute to the efforts undertaken by the Bureau of Energy Efficiency (BEE). The Ministry of Environment and Forests (MoEF) has designed the Energy Conservation Building Code (ECBC) and a technical manual for environmental appraisal of buildings. The National Electricity Policy, 2001 highlights the need for the use of decentralized renewable energy technologies. Promotion of renewable energy is the task of the Ministry of New and Renewable Sources (MNRE) along with the Indian Renewable Energy Development Agency Ltd. (IREDA). The National Urban Transport Policy promotes public transport over personal vehicles and favours clean fuels such as CNG.

In 2008, India adopted its National Action Plan on Climate Change.[40] The opening sentence of the Action Plan captures the central dilemma: "India is faced with the challenge of sustaining its rapid economic growth while dealing with the global threat of climate change."[41] The objectives of India's strategy, as identified by the Plan are *i)* to adapt to climate change and *ii)* to enhance ecological sustainability of India's development path. The Action Plan stresses the idea of 'per capita emission': "the principle of equity that must underlie the global approach must allow each inhabitant of the earth an equal entitlement to the global atmospheric resource". It further makes the claim that "its per capita greenhouse gas emissions will at no point exceed that of developed countries even as we pursue our development objectives."[42] In elaborating the principles that are to govern its policy, the document states:

"Maintaining a high growth rate is essential for increasing living standards of the vast majority of our people and reducing their vulnerability to the impacts of climate change." The proclaimed approach of the Plan is the facilitation of a directional shift in the development pathway; it identifies measures that promote developmental objectives while also addressing climate change. The Plan includes eight national missions representing strategies for achieving climate change goals: solar; enhanced energy efficiency; sustainable habitat; water; sustaining the Himalayan ecosystem; 'Green India'; sustainable agriculture and strategic knowledge for climate change.

Although the broad intention of the National Action Plan has been lauded in some quarters, it has also been criticized as being 'high-sounding' and 'vague' and shying away from real commitments. It has been pointed out that the Action plan sets very few quantitative targets or concrete timetables. India's climate policy making in general has also come under fire. It has been alleged that

> India's climate policy is made in isolation from the people by a bureaucratic cabal, excluding independent experts and representatives of civil society, leave alone those most affected by climate change.... Yet, most opinion-shapers treat climate change not as a survival or development/equity issue, but as a diplomatic one, with sovereignty separated from the people. Our people need a strong, equitable climate deal.... This won't happen unless people's movements seize the climate agenda.[43]

Collaborative Efforts on Climate Change: EU and India

India-EU relations go back a long way. In the early 1960s, India became one of the first countries to establish diplomatic relations with the (then) EEC. In 1994, the cooperation agreement signed between EU and India expanded bilateral relations beyond trade and economic cooperation. Since the first India-EU Summit in Lisbon in June 2000, summit-level interactions have become an annual feature. In November 2004,

India-EU relations were upgraded to the level of a 'strategic partnership'.[44]

An important question to be asked from the perspective of EU-India relations is the potential for cooperation and collaboration between the EU and India in the area of climate change. India and EU are projected as natural allies based on a host of commonalities.[45] It would be pertinent to see how far these commonalities can be channelized to apply to climate change. EU-India relations have been embodied in the EU-India annual bilateral summits,[46] which have been held since 2000 and has focused on a gamut of important issues of concern to both actors. In the 6 November 2009 annual summit held at New Delhi, climate change was one of the major issues discussed.[47] The European Commission and India recently launched a Euro 10 million joint research programme in the field of solar energy.[48] European Commission President Jose Manuel Barroso stated in the context of climate change at the eve of the summit that "we are ready to help if developing countries and, in particular, emerging economies like India deliver".[49] It was also made clear that climate change and energy would be prominent on the year's summit agenda and that there would be concrete action in the field of energy efficiency, clean coal technology and renewable energy. The EU and India already share strong ties in the field of science and technology, India being the third largest recipient of R&D projects funded by the EU. These ties can be further streamlined to focus on climate change related technology.

Areas for cooperation between the EU and India need to be identified. Some areas suggested by a note prepared for the European Parliament[50] include those of water management (watershed management, rainwater harvesting and groundwater recharge), flood control, health, agriculture, rural development, and insurance schemes for the poor. For mitigation-related activities, improving efficiency of coal-based power plants, promoting renewable energy and modifying the transportation sector to make it more efficient, are all areas in which the European experience can prove beneficial to Indian conditions.

The EU-India Strategic Partnership and the Joint Action Plan are steps towards cooperation between the two actors. Although there exists an institutionalized mechanism for bilateral ties, the relationship has been disproportionately focused on markets and trade. There lies a wealth of potential in deepening ties by focusing on issues of climate change bilaterally. Considering the deep interest and involvement of both actors in acting to address climate change and also considering the wide implications of climate change on all other policy areas, this issues area must be consciously nurtured as one where the spotlight of bilateral engagement falls.

Cooperation with third countries is an identified course of action in EU policy. "Climate change calls for revisiting and reinforcing EU cooperation and political dialogue instruments, giving more attention to the impact of climate change on security." A possible action identified in the paper is examining the security implication of climate change in dialogue with third counties including through sharing of analyses.[51]

More specifically, in the area of research, there is much to be gained from bilateral cooperation. The EU recognizes that

> In developing countries a range of barriers – including lack of policies, information and capacities – hampers the development, transfer and deployment of technologies for adaptation and mitigation. Cooperation between developed and developing countries on R&D is essential to achieving common technology goals, and the EU is committed to working with developing countries to explore how joint research efforts can be taken forward...[52]

Thus, in promoting R&D that can form the basis for mitigation and adaptation action, collaborative bilateral action is of potential value.

Conclusions

Although climate change as an issue is of global concern,

perspectives, perceptions, and policies on climate change differ widely across the world. As is clear even from a discussion of two actors in the global arena – the European Union and India – divergences are clearly noticeable. At the international level, both have articulated a commitment to the cause of combating climate change and both have been active participants in the climate regime. Yet the implications of the regime and the nature of their participation vary considerably. There is a high level of acceptability in the European Union regarding the need for strict action to control climate change. The domestic action undertaken by the Union in terms of emissions reduction, which is exemplary by global standards, indicates the serious commitment of the region towards combating climate change. International and domestic policies of the EU reflect the high priority and acceptability that climate change receives as a policy area. The EU has clearly enunciated its willingness to undertake deep cuts but has also underscored the need for emerging economies like India to come on board for overall emissions reduction efforts. It is under the EU's leadership that the "agreement to agree" was reached at Durban in 2011, where the EU managed to achieve it long-term objective of bringing Annex II countries also under the obligations of legal commitments.

India's stance in the international climate regime has been somewhat different, stemming from the fact that its position is dissimilar to the EU within the regime. Benefiting from its non-Annex I status, India wished to retain its exemption from legally binding emission targets even in the post-Kyoto scenario. Its fierce resistance to internationally imposed commitments is contrary to the EU's view of the need to bind India with quantifiable targets. The confrontation between EU and India at Durban was a manifestation of this divergence. India does however offer domestic, self-imposed targets, which it will meet through clean energy policies and a change in its development trajectory. Policies such as the National Action Plan on Climate

Change are indicative of its commitment to climate change action.

Domestic action undertaken by the EU and India is also qualitatively very different. Whereas the EU domestic policy establishes clear-cut quantifiable targets relating to several schemes that have already been implemented, the Indian situation banks on climate change action incidentally resulting from policies designed for other objectives. The specific action plan that it has recently adopted is bereft of specific targets and timetables. The fact that the objective of the national action plan makes no mention of emission reduction but emphasizes the need for sustaining growth in order to equip its poor clearly indicate the difference in emphasis between the policies of the EU and India.

The divergences in perspectives and policies on climate change result from the differing perceptions prevailing in the two economies. Because the two actors occupy different positions in Maslow's 'hierarchy of needs pyramid', they exhibit vastly different perceptions of their respective development priorities. The areas of convergence are therefore not too wide. Common concerns such as enhancing research potential relating to climate change can be productively addressed through investing in bilateral cooperative action, specifically in relation to research and clean technology. The focus should be on working around differences and building on convergences, which are most likely to be found in the bilateral strategic relationship between EU and India.

Although efforts to promote convergences are certainly worthwhile, the reality of the current situation seems to indicate a growing chasm between the two players. The European Union and India have a significant role to play in contributing to climate change control. Additionally, the stakes are high for both actors and therefore a high level of political involvement at both ends in likely. The stress that was visible between India and the EU at Durban regarding the terminology of the proposed agreement already indicates the roughness of the road ahead till 2015. Moreover, India finds itself in formal opposition to the EU's recently announced emissions tax on airlines. In the immediate years ahead, the EU-India interaction is more likely to be marked by friction than by a convergent approach. It is hoped that the larger cause of addressing climate change does not suffer in the process.

NOTES

1 Opening Clause of the Preamble to the Draft Decision -/CP.17 on *Establishment of an Ad Hoc Working Group on the Durban Platform for Enhanced Action* adopted at the Durban Conference in December 2011 [FCCC/CP/2011/L.10, 10 December 2011], http://unfccc.int/resource/docs/2011/cop17/eng/l10.pdf.

2 The 17th Conference of Parties (COP 17) of the *United Nations Framework Convention on Climate Change* took place from 28 November to 9 December 2011 in Durban, South Africa.

3 The President of COP17/CMP7 Maite Nkoana-Mashabane said: "What we have achieved in Durban will play a central role in saving tomorrow, today." See UNFCCC official website at http://unfccc.int/meetings/durban_nov_2011/meeting/6245.php.

4 The expected outcome at Copenhagen was the adoption of a new Protocol to replace the Kyoto Protocol once it lapsed in 2012. But what began as 'Hopenhagen' was later variously termed as 'Nopenhagen', 'Flopenhagen' and 'Tokenhagen', See "The Opinion Pages," *The New York Times*, 24 December 2009, at http://schott.blogs.nytimes.com/2009/12/24/nopenhagen-flopenhagen/.

5 The 15th Conference of Parties (COP 15) of the *United Nations Framework Convention on Climate Change* (UNFCCC) was held at Copenhagen, Denmark from 7 to 19 December 2009.

6 United Nations, *United Nations Framework Convention on Climate Change* (1992) [FCCC/INFORMAL/84, GE.05-62220 (E) 200705], http://unfccc.int/resource/docs/convkp/conveng.pdf.

7 United Nations, *Kyoto Protocol to the United Nations Framework Convention on Climate Change* (1997), http://unfccc.int/resource/docs/convkp/kpeng.pdf.

8 Article 3(1) of the Kyoto Protocol: "The Parties included in Annex I shall, individually or jointly, ensure that their aggregate anthropogenic

carbon dioxide equivalent emissions of the greenhouse gases listed in Annex A do not exceed their assigned amounts, calculated pursuant to their quantified emission limitation and reduction commitments inscribed in Annex B and in accordance with the provisions of this Article, with a view to *reducing their overall emissions of such gases by at least 5 per cent below 1990 levels in the commitment period 2008 to 2012* (emphasis added)."

9 Preamble to the UNFCCC: "*Acknowledging* that the global nature of climate change calls for the widest possible cooperation by all countries and their participation in an effective and appropriate international response, in accordance with their common but differentiated responsibilities..." Further, commitments imposed on Parties to the UNFCCC under Article 4 are to "...tak[e] into account their common but differentiated responsibilities..."

10 The Kyoto mechanisms – Emissions Trading, Joint Implementation and Clean Development Mechanism – allow for flexibility in meeting emission reduction commitments if they cannot be met purely by domestic action. As part of the 'carbon market' set up under the Emissions Trading mechanism (Article 17), parties with emission reduction commitments are assigned targets for the 2008-2012 commitment period and if countries have spare emission units, they can sell their excess units to other committed countries that are likely to cross their target. A country with emission reduction targets may earn emission reduction units by implementing emission-reduction projects in other countries – it can do so in another Annex I country [Joint Implementation (Article 6)] or in a developing country [Clean Development Mechanism (Article 12)].

11 The second biggest carbon emitter remained notably absent from the Kyoto regime, refusing to be bound by the commitments imposed by the Protocol. The US administration made it clear that it would not be signatory to any protocol that *i)* did not include binding targets and timetables for developing countries as well or *ii)* that would result in 'serious harm' to the American economy. Despite the non-participation of the largest emitter, the Kyoto Protocol entered into force in 2005 when Russia ratified it, fulfilling the legal requirements for entry into force. While Australia – the other major long-time non-member – came on board in December 2007 (ratification of the Kyoto Protocol was the first official act of the new Kevin Rudd government), the US continues to remain outside the sphere of operation of the Protocol.

12 Nicholas Stern, *Stern Review: The Economics of Climate Change*, http://

siteresources.worldbank.org/INTINDONESIA/Resources/

13 IPCC, *Climate Change 2007: Synthesis Report*, http://www.ipcc.ch/pdf/assessment-report/ar4/syr/ar4_syr.pdf.

14 The Bali Action Plan, adopted in COP 13 at Bali, set out a framework for negotiating a second phase of Kyoto, focusing on four main issues – mitigation; adaptation; technology development and transfer; and financial resources and investment. More importantly, countries decided to reach an 'agreed outcome' – in all likelihood a legally binding treaty to be christened 'Copenhagen Protocol' to replace the Kyoto Protocol – by the end of 2009 at Copenhagen. See United Nations, *Bali Action Plan*, Decision -/CP.13, http://unfccc.int/files/meetings/cop_13/application/pdf/cp_bali_action.pdf.

15 The controversial 'Australian proposal', floated in October 2009 and backed by the EU and US, had floated the idea of a single listing of all countries and *similar* commitments though of *varying degrees* and did not carry a contingent guarantee of technology or finance. Termed the "murder of the Kyoto Protocol" by India, the proposal was criticized for running counter to the very spirit of the Kyoto Protocol by putting the knife of 'single listing' through the heart of the principle of common but differentiated responsibilities.

16 United Nations, *Copenhagen Accord*, Decision -/CP.15, http://unfccc.int/files/meetings/cop_15/application/pdf/cop15_cph_auv.pdf.

17 Praful Bidwai. "Copenhagen Cop Out," *Hindustan Times*, 30 December 2009.

18 This would require a peak by 2020 and then a reduction by at least 50 per cent of 1990 levels by 2050.

19 See John Vidal and Fiona Harvey, "Climate deal salvaged after marathon talks in Durban," *The Observer*, 11 December 2011, http://www.guardian.co.uk/environment/2011/dec/10/un-climate-change-summit-durban.

20 Ibid.

21 See R. Ramachandran, "Uncertain Stand," *Frontline*, 28(27), 31 December 2011-13 January 2012.

22 Ibid.

23 This is equivalent to 1.2 degrees Celsius above today's temperature.

24 European Commission (2009) *Climate Change*, http://ec.europa.eu/environment/pubs/pdf/factsheets/climate_change.pdf.

25 EU Memo, *The Copenhagen Climate Conference: Key EU Objectives*, MEMO/09/534, 2 December 2009.

26 European Commission (2009), *EU Action Against Climate Change: Leading*

Global Action to 2020 and Beyond, p. 9.

27 As per the version made public by the media, the letter expressed concern about India being seen as a 'deal-breaker'. It diluted India's stance demanding finance and technology as compensation from developed countries and underscored that "...we need to mitigate in self-interest". It suggested that India allow scrutiny of even those emissions control steps that it takes under its own legislation and at its cost (like IMF surveillance and WTO TPRM). The letter also asserted that the Australian proposal would cause no harm to India as long as it recognizes differences in obligations. Needless to say, the Minister's letter stirred up a hornet's nest, although he later claimed that his communication had been totally distorted and the Prime Minister's Office also clarified that there was to be no shift in the Indian negotiating stance.

28 "India Should Accept Climate Change Flow Obligations, Ask for Superfund: Jagdish Bhagwati," *The Hindu*, 12 August 2009.

29 Breaking the Climate Deadlock," *The Hindu*, 23 June 2009.

30 This target has been arrived at by the Planning Commission based on research.

31 European Commission, *Climate Change and International Security* [Paper from the High Representative and the European Commission to the European Council] S113/08, 14 March 2008, http://www.consilium.europa.eu/uedocs/cms_data/docs/pressdata/en/reports/99387.pdf, p. 2. The Report concludes that it is in Europe's self-interest to address the security implications of climate change.

32 For details of the ECCP, see European Commission (2006), *The European Climate Change Programme: EU Action Against Climate Change*, http://ec.europa.eu/environment/climat/pdf/eu_climate_change_progr.pdf.

33 European Commission (2009), *EU Action Against Climate Change: Leading Global Action to 2020 and Beyond*, p. 10.

34 For details, see European Commission (2008), *EU Action Against Climate Change: The EU Emissions Trading Scheme*, http://ec.europa.eu/environment/climat/pdf/brochures/ets_en.pdf.

35 European Commission (2009), *EU Action Against Climate Change: Leading Global Action to 2020 and Beyond*, p. 12. http://ec.europa.eu/environment/climat/pdf/brochures/post_2012_en.pdf.

36 Carbon capture and sequestration technology entails the capture of emitted carbon dioxide and storage underground so that it does not lead to global warming.

37 European Commission, n. 35, p. 14.

38 Government of India, *India: Addressing Energy Security and Climate Change*, 2007 http://envfor.nic.in/divisions/ccd/Addressing_CC_09-10-07.pdf pp. 5-6. Also see European Parliament (2008), *Climate Change and India: Impacts, Policy Responses and a Framework for EU-India Cooperation*, [DG Internal Policies of the Union, Note, IP/A/CLIM/NT/2007-10, PE 400.991], p. 1.

39 Government of India, Ministry of Environment and Forests, *National Environment Policy, 2006*, http://www.envfor.nic.in/nep/nep2006.html. Also, for an overview of India's actions at the domestic level on climate change, see Government of India, Ministry of Environment and Forests (2004), *India's Initial National Communication to the United Nations Framework Convention on Climate Change*, http://unfccc.int/resource/docs/natc/indnc1.pdf and Government of India (2008) *India's Second National Communication to the United Nations Framework Convention on Climate Change*, http://www.natcomindia.org/brochure5.pdf.

40 Government of India, Prime Minister's Council on Climate Change, *National Action Plan on Climate Change*, 2008. http://pmindia.nic.in/Pg01-52.pdf.

41 Ibid., p. 1.

42 Ibid., p. 2.

43 Praful Bidwai, "Copenhagen Cop Out," *Hindustan Times*, 30 December 2009.

44 *The India-EU Strategic Partnership Joint Action Plan*, 7 September 2005, http://commerce.nic.in/india-EU-jap.pdf, p. 1.

45 "India and the EU, as the largest democracies in the world, share common values and beliefs that make them natural partners as well as factors of stability in the present world order. We share a common commitment to democracy, pluralism, human rights and the rule of law, to an independent judiciary and media. India and the EU also have much to contribute towards fostering a rule-based international order – be it through the United Nations (UN) or through the World Trade Organisation (WTO). We hold a common belief in the fundamental importance of multilateralism in accordance with the UN Charter and in the essential role of the UN for maintaining international peace and security, promoting the economic and social advancement of all peoples and meeting global threats and challenges." The India-EU Strategic Partnership Joint Action Plan, 7 September 2005, http://commerce.nic.in/india-EU-jap.pdf, p. 1.

46 The EU-India Annual Summit provides, since 2000, a platform for

political dialogue between the two actors. In 2004, a concrete strategic partnership was established. A Joint Action Plan, adopted in 2005 and revised in 2008, has further reinforced bilateral ties.

47 Other issues included energy security, terrorism, and regional security.

48 The solar energy proposal involves a funding of Euro 5 million from each side.

49 EU Press release, *The EU-India Summit to Focus on Climate Change, Energy and Trade*, IP/09/1678, 5 November 2009, http://europa.eu/rapid/pressReleasesAction.do?reference=IP/09/1678&format=HTML&aged=0&language=EN&guiLanguage=en.

50 European Parliament, *Climate Change and India: Impacts, Policy Responses and a Framework for EU-India Cooperation,* 2008 [DG Internal Policies of the Union, Note, IP/A/CLIM/NT/2007-10, PE 400.991].

51 European Commission, *Climate Change and International Security* [Paper from the High Representative and the European Commission to the European Council] S113/08, 14 March 2008, p. 11.

52 European Commission (2009), *EU Action Against Climate Change: Leading Global Action to 2020 and Beyond*, http://ec.europa.eu/environment/climat/pdf/brochures/post_2012_en.pdf, p. 30.

Index